MW00380821

Born to be me

The Sisterhood *folios*:
BORN TO BE ME

© 2017 by CREATIVE PUBLISHING GROUP

Published by CREATIVE PUBLISHING GROUP

All rights reserved. No part of this book may be reproduced in any form or by any electronic or mechanical means, or the facilitation thereof, including information storage and retrieval systems, without permission in writing from the publisher. Except by a reviewer, who may quote brief passages in a review.

The views and opinions expressed are those of the authors. Although the author and publisher have made every effort to make sure all information is correct at press time, the author and publisher do not assume and hereby disclaim any liability to any party for any loss, damage, disruptions caused by stories with this book, whether such information is a result of errors or emission, accident, slander or other cause.

For any information regarding permission contact
info@creativepublishinggroup.com
www.creativepublishinggroup.com

ISBN 978-0-9958810-6-8

Printed in the United States of America
First publication, 2017.

Design: Amir Saarony

The Sisterhood *folios*

Born to be me

Creative
PUBLISHING GROUP

Acknowledgments

TINA AURELIO

Yea, though I walk through the valley of the shadow of death,
I fear no evil, For Thou art with me;
Surely goodness and mercy shall follow me all the days of my
life. ~Psalm 23.

DARCIE BOLAND

This chapter would not have been possible if I had lost faith,
it is with my deepest gratitude that I have been blessed with
my two precious children who never gave up on me, even
when things seemed so dark. I owe the strength for putting
these words down on paper to the creator of the Travelling
Sisterhood Group and the amazing ladies in there. My journey
through relationship healing and understanding myself with
Theresa Vigarino, Soul Essence Alchemist who has guided me
and taught me that with God all things are possible.

ANGELA CATENARO MCNEILL

Thank you to my loving husband, Michael, for always
encouraging me to BE ME. Elliot and James, thank you for
choosing me to be your mom and for helping me to free
my voice. Thank you to the butterflies who lift me and to
the lions who shoved me-you all inspire me to be the best
version of me.

LUCIA COLANGELO

To my sons, Jesse and Marco, my nieces Sabrina and Julia, my Father and my Mama in heaven, we are all linked together by our hearts. To my wonderful family and friends, thank you for the love, guidance, support, many bottles of wine, lattes, pizza and road trips!

LAURA DEGASPERIS

I would like to thank my husband, Mike for his ongoing support. To my daughter, Emily, you inspire me to pursue my passion every day. To my family who allow me to be who I am and support me. To all my friends who have been there for me during my struggles, I thank you all.

LAUREN DICKSON

I would like to thank my sisters for keeping me sane with all of our crazy laughter. Also for all of your love and support, and your beautiful hearts and personalities which truly make my heart smile! To my brothers; we didn't always get along or connect well, but in our adult years, despite some ups and downs, we have connected and loved each other. I love my big bros! To my niece, who brings a ray of light into my life on a daily basis! You are already an incredible child, and quickly growing into an even more beautifully intelligent and amazing young woman! Finally, to God, for giving me the strength and wisdom to fight my toughest battles and embrace everything you give to me.

MARTHA ELEFTHERIOU

For my mother Elli, who taught me how to pray and how to love unconditionally. A heartfelt thank you to my husband, Michael, for all your love and support in helping me reach my dreams. To my daughters, Aliyah and Chantelle, you are the greatest blessings I could have ever wished for. Thank you for choosing me as your mother!

ELAINE ESPINOLA

It is with admiration and sincere gratitude that I thank my husband, Billy Keltz, for encouraging me in every way, at every turn in the magical maze of life and adventure. Beyond support, you offer guidance, direction and sound advice. My happiness has always been your happiness and I am one very lucky lady. To my late father, Dr. Jesse T. Espinola, whose quiet observation of the world around him, inspired mine.

PINA FERRARO

Mom and Dad, I am, because you are my foundation, my will, my being my home and eternal love.Jonathan my son, my gift from God, my pride and greatest accomplishment in life, love you forever.To Creative Publishing Group/Carol Starr Taylor, for the blessing of believing in me, when I didn't believe in myself.

JEN HECHT

My chapter is dedicated to my dad, Richard Clack for the sacrifices he made for me to achieve my dreams over the years. He taught me that life will be filled with potholes and uneven pavement but how you adapt and pivot will determine how you show up in the world.
Thank you for being awesome, Ricky. I love you.

NIKKI-MONIQUE KURNATH

THANK YOU to: Carol, Amir and the Sisters within Creative Publishing Group, many leaders who inspire me and special friends that encourage me. To my parents– Cyril and Janine, my siblings– Renea & Michael and the rest of my extended family in Poland, Canada and the U.S. Thanks to my special guys– Blappy Nate, Big Bro Stephen and Bestie Bro Jordan. And to my greatest gift and true love of my life– Thank You to my amazing son Dylan. I'm blessed being your mommy and daddy. My chapter is dedicated to the memories of my youthful friend Francesca and my loving grandparents Dziadzia and Babcia Solski. Kocham cie XO

APRIL NICOLAS

Grateful to my family Chris, Ariana, Mateo and Luna, you are my greatest treasures. Blessed enough to be guided by the most amazing Spirit of life and love always reminding me that I am never alone, that I am surrounded by my angels from heaven and here on earth.

MALI PHONPADITH

I am incredibly blessed to have an amazing family and wonderful friends. I would like to acknowledge all the beautiful souls who have graced my life and showed me how to experience wonder, hope, joy, passion, peace and love.

I would like to especially thank my husband, Victor Cora Nazario, my mother and father, Keonoukane and Sivone (in memoriam), my grandmother, Khamkong (in memoriam), Mina, Lola, Soudara, Ong, Lucy (my siblings), Luz (my mother-in-law), Victor (my father-in-law), Hunter, Jaden, Reuben, Grace (my niece and nephews), aunts, uncles, cousins, McCarty family, Khamvongsa family, Souvandara family, Prasavath family, Rubio family, Meehan family, Rajapakse family, Mounkhaty family, Narvaez family, dear friends, and my powerful mentors. Thank you for showing me the way and offering light and hope in times of darkness and despair. I have no idea where I would be today without your guidance and love. I'm grateful to be here, living a life of passion and purpose.

KIM REDMAN

I would like to thank my family for coming to this Earth walk and sharing my lessons.

I would like to thank the Divine for giving me such a clear and passionate purpose.

Mostly, I would thank to my husband, mate, and business partner; Mike. You are my rock.

Thanks for always bringing me home, back to my heart.

TERESA SCIANI

To my daughter Julia who inspires me with her strength, my son Andrew who has taught me surrender and my husband Jerry my biggest fan.

Thank you, Carol Starr Taylor for this incredible opportunity to share my story of how "I was born to be me." This chapter would not have been possible without learning from the past.

SARAH SHAKESPEARE

Sarah would like to thank her husband Paul and their three daughters Abigail, Hannah and Emily-Jane for helping her to see that 24hrs in a day can be used very productively! Their love and support has allowed Sarah to be exactly where she is supposed to be today. She would also like to thank Ben Kimberley and Kathy Maier for giving her the opportunities that have helped her excel in her life. She will be eternally grateful because these two amazing people saw something in her before she even did.

CAROL STARR TAYLOR

To my beautiful children– I am so proud of the young men you have become. To the Authors in The Sisterhood Folios, past, present and future, I honor your strength, love and courage to share and inspire. To all of you, who inspire and/or teach me lessons each and everyday, I am truly grateful.

DENISE K VENUTO

For my daughters. Never give up!

HEATHER WILSON

I would like to thank my friends who believed in me, stuck by me no matter what. My mom and dad, I love you forever. My husband, Jamie, who has been my biggest supporter, fan and has taught me true unconditional love. To my three beautiful children, you are my world and my "Why." Thank you for all of your support and love, as we moved through various changes together. My mother and father in-law, your love and support has been incredible and clearly has shone through your amazing children, Alexa and Jamie. I love you all so much. Thank you to Carol Starr Taylor as well, for this opportunity and to all of you, co-author peeps – your encouragement and support has been so heartwarming.

Table of Contents

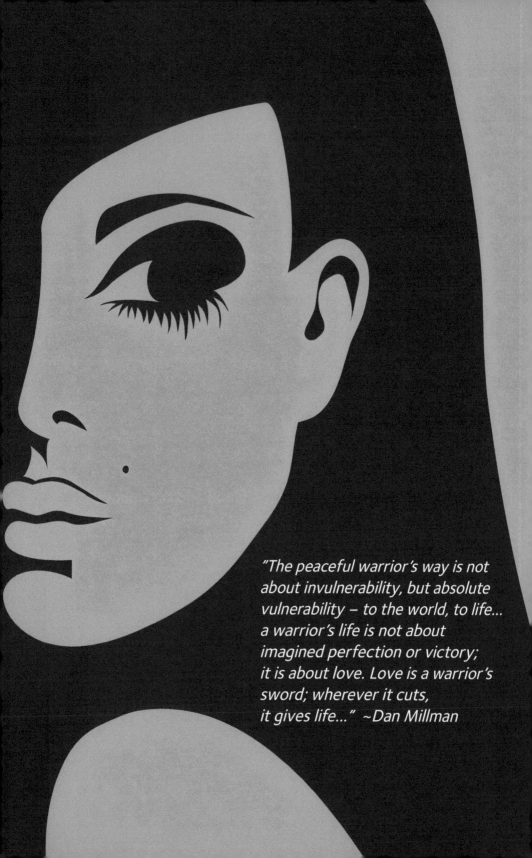

"The peaceful warrior's way is not about invulnerability, but absolute vulnerability – to the world, to life... a warrior's life is not about imagined perfection or victory; it is about love. Love is a warrior's sword; wherever it cuts, it gives life..." ~Dan Millman

Maimah Karmo

Foreword

I'm honored to write this Foreword for **The Sisterhood *folios*: Born to Be Me**. The women who have shared their stories here bare everything– gifting us with powerful lessons of faith, gratitude, compassion and healing. Now sisters through their common narrative, I know their stories will inspire every reader to become even more fearless in pursuit of her soul's purpose. I could think of only one word that kept resonating with me as I read these women stories... and that word is "fearless"!!!

Freedom. These women's stories talk about the importance of exercising the freedom to be ourselves and focusing on our highest life path. We must always live in emotional, mental and spiritual freedom, standing up for ourselves, and allowing our spirits to be wild and free.

Endless Possibilities Exist. Live in prayer and focus on spirituality. Life will bring us challenges, but when we focus on our spiritual practices daily, integrating gratitude, stillness, silence and divine connection, endless possibilities exist.

Awakening. Sometimes in life we forget who we are, and then we lose ourselves. We get wrapped up in the world and sometimes "fall asleep." These amazing women pushed past family challenges, unhealthy patterns, and found the courage to build the lives they wanted.

Return to Love. No matter what, we must always choose love, for we are warriors, and love is the warrior's sword!

Life Decisions. Every single decision we make sends energy out into the Universe. These amazing women recognized that and made intentional choices to create joy, happiness, fulfillment and abundance, bringing into their lives the things they desired.

Every moment matters. Every moment matters, the peaks and the valleys. They all shape the mosaic of our lives. We can take the lesson from each, and find beauty even in the brokenness.

Self-Love. Our experience of life changes when we love ourselves first. The catalysts for each woman came after she had an "aha" moment, where, through self reflection and practicing radical self-love, she reclaimed herself.

Strength. We find strength by appreciating the lessons learned when things were falling apart. Every roadblock brings us closer to the truth of who we really are at our core– "love."

In each of these women, we see a bit of ourselves, transforming, spiritually evolving, and as we soar, lifting each other up. Each of these women are living fearlessly, empowering other women with the belief that they too, can pursue their soul's purpose and give birth to their truth.

Maimah Karmo is a mother, philanthropist, author, advocate, cancer warrior, magazine publisher, life coach, entrepreneur, empath, badass and unicorn. Maimah's story began in Liberia, West Africa, where she was born. After surviving two wars in Liberia, during a third coup d'état, she fled to the United States at 15 years old with her family.

She worked her way through college and created her version of the American Dream.

At the age of 32, Maimah was raising a beautiful 3-year-old when she was diagnosed with aggressive breast cancer in 2006. While in treatment, Maimah made a promise to God that if she survived, she would create an organization to educate, empower, advocate for and support young women affected by breast cancer. Her promise became the Tigerlily Foundation. She is also the author of Fearless: Awakening to My Life's Purpose Through Breast Cancer; and Publisher of Bliss Magazine. Maimah has been featured on The Oprah Winfrey Show, OWN Network, The Today Show, Good Morning America, MSNBC, in Cosmopolitan Magazine, Essence, Marie Claire, Redbook and more. Maimah loves empowering others, through speaking engagements and life coaching.

Visit Maimahkarmo.com to learn more about her coaching, register for her next "I Manifest Bliss Experience" event, and to subscribe to her podcast, Pure Bliss.

A Return to Love

It has been two years since my eighteen-year-old son Michael, passed away from a drug addiction. In that time, I have made a conscious decision to heal and move forward from the "hellish" state that his death sent me spiraling down into. In writing this, I am forced to look back and go deeper into my feelings, which I am finding to be an immensely painful task. I am remembering so many years of laughing, crying, loving, hurting, joy and pain. The last four years of Michael's life my emotions were a full out battle between fear and love. Looking back at it now it has been a journey of my spiritual awakening with all the privileges of love, faith, miracles and God.

On one hand looking back and realizing where I am today, it's a miracle that I am still breathing. My son Michael was my baby; when he passed on I left with him. My whole world was shattered and, along with a broken heart I no longer had a place in this world. On the other hand, in his short life,

Michael was and remains my greatest teacher. For me, Michael became "Michael the Great Awakener." He showed me the beauty of his existence in heaven, and made me see the same beauty that has always been here on earth. For that I am eternally grateful. In search of your heaven Michael, I have found my own.

I am looking out at the world wondering where all this time has gone— one foot on either side of the divide between where I've been and where I have left to go. But maybe I have never had this much to look back on. I've always said that if I ever felt I'd truly achieved it all, and I have arrived, it would be time for me to leave and rest in my Eternal Home.

It was early Wednesday morning, I believed I was dreaming when my son Michael's life flat lined on the monitor. It was not real! This was not what I had chosen for my beautiful boy with a golden heart. I remember the nurse calling Michael's time of death. I felt my heart split into pieces and I could only think; I am not going to make it. My heart was torn and I wanted only one thing. To be with my beautiful son. Nowhere else would ever be tolerable.

"God, please help me, bring Michael back to me!" My prayer did not come in form of an answer to my plea: Instead I entered a state of utter stillness. I had a direct and profound experience of oneness, an unbreakable connection between myself, my son Michael and all living things, seen and unseen. For the first time in my life, I felt "freedom" from my ever-present internal war.

Nothing can fill the gap when we are away from those we love, and it would be wrong to try. It would be easy, wouldn't it, to somehow close down the valves of love so we couldn't be hurt this much again? For a while I felt numbness, I was lost, I couldn't get my bearings, I felt like I didn't belong. But without the love of God, I would not have made it through this time of grieving.

Love calls to love. I was summoned to my grief by love, and I am healed by love. I believe I will not be healed, if I do not participate, if I do not answer to the love of others by my love for them. Yes, it takes risk and courage to love again. It is my courage that affirms the love I share with Michael.

If there is one thing I know that I can share with others who may be going through their own grief it is how changeable my moods can be. One moment I am relatively calm, in control, keeping my grief at bay. The next moment, I am overwhelmed, my equilibrium is shattered. Anything can send me off– a fragrance, the words of a song, an article in the newspaper that reminds me of my Michael. The first sign of spring and my son is not here to share it. Even Mother's Day sent me reeling in a vortex of sadness, pain and suffering.

I sometimes wonder about my sanity. When will my moods be more measured so I am not always in danger of being swept away, of falling through the trapdoor of despair? My life has been shattered by loss, I realize that it will take time for the pieces to come together again. I am patient and loving with myself, honoring the moods, the pain, the good or bad of my grieving. I trust, I am on my way to being healed.

I have started picking up the pieces, and the strength to rebuild my life. It is strangely reassuring– this suggestion that the pain of that empty space will always be with me. Because while I do want to feel better, I do not want to ever to forget my son.

I believe my ability to love and care for the world is not limited. It does not mean that taking on a new love means replacing an old one. Time does not expand, but love does. What was once loved and cherished is not replaceable. But in allowing myself to love again, I am starting to feel whole again.

I want you to know that we do not get over the loss of a loved one. I know that once Michael passed on out of this physical world and into the world of the spiritual, I realize that I cannot experience him as I once knew. But I can always experience him in my life by keeping his memory alive in my mind and in my heart. I realize that Michael is a spiritual being, not limited to physical properties. He is with me and around me more than ever before. Knowing that makes life seem possible once again.

I will always be 'Michael's Mom'. When Michael grew into a young man, he made choices that I did not approve of. The last four years of Michael's life where tough and hard to endure. I never stopped loving him. He showed me to accept him and love him just as he was. We never stop being parents even though our children choose a different life path. For my whole life, I will love Michael and all his heart and think about him every day.

Falling in love with you Michael was always easy. Our short time together was always filled with love, laughter, joy, anger and tears. It is when you want to be together despite it all, I discovered my Eternal Love for you! – Momma.

Michael was born on Monday, June 10, 1996. He greeted his parents and the world with a peaceful smile. Instead of cries of protest at the bright lights and all the faces looking down at him, he seemed content of his surroundings. I had a very easy pregnancy with Michael, no morning sickness, and he never kept me up at night. He joyfully grew in my womb without making a fuss.

I referred to Michael as a "cherub." My term of endearment for him was "cotton ball." He would only cry when he needed to be fed and changed, and amused himself by marveling at his surroundings. Self-sufficient always, he insisted on managing everything on his own.

His love for life and nature was beyond measure. He took care of everyone and everything without being asked. Michael had a "golden heart." He was a kind, gentle, fun loving, happy-go-lucky child. He was well liked by everyone who came in contact with him. No question about it.

It was no surprise when Michael started junior kindergarten that he went to school joyfully each day. No complaints, no kicking and screaming. I often wondered how blessed of a mom I was. It was unbelievable how this child would never cause any trouble or complain about anything.

Life was just easy with Michael; it was just that way. As he grew older, Michael demonstrated unconditional love for children. He loved to tell stories, play with them, but his favorite was to read to them. He never lost his patience. Come to think of it, Michael never lost his patience with anyone. A pillar of strength and a great listener he was everyone's go-to guy. He had all the answers and solutions for all his friends. He was always available to extend his help to anyone. He was everyone's number one fan.

When Michael was six years old, I separated from Michael's dad, after seventeen years of marriage. It was a brutal custody battle, Michael and I were separated for a full-year before we reunited again. When I got Michael back it was on part-time basis. Michael was heartbroken. I have always felt that the divorce affected Michael deeply. I believe that children do not have a way of accepting and living the reality that has been dealt by their parents. I also believe that it impacted Michael to the point of escaping his emotions towards his family life.

When Michael started High School, everything changed. He became quieter at home, withdrawn from our family, he no longer joined in family gatherings, he always had other plans. He had nothing much to say most of the time. "Shoulders shrugging" was his way of communicating.

Everyone was telling me it was just a phase, but as time passed it became apparent to me that something else was going on, a mother always knows. His behavior was the first change I noticed. He used to care so much and then he never cared at all. He also became demanding and rude when he did not get his way.

It became difficult to get him to get up and be present to his life. For example, getting up for school was devastating. I dreaded when the clock went off at 7:00 a.m. We would argue every morning. After all the fighting, he would finally get up. He would get mouthy and belligerent each time. He had no patience and his aggression became worse as time passed.

Another change was that he could not commit or keep appointments. He always stood me up or kept me waiting forever. I also noticed that he would tell me where to pick him up and then he would phone me and tell me it would be somewhere else. And then come up with an amazing story (fiction) as to what happened. It was so exhausting just to listen to him sometimes. I just wanted to say to him, "I don't want to know, honey." or "you are ok, and it is good enough for me."

I would get calls from his Principal, advising me that Michael did not show up to 1st period. I was so naïve and I would always say to him, "It's not possible, I just dropped him off!" I also noticed he was asking for a lot of money, all the time. Excuses galore for what he had to do with it. Lying now became second nature. I recall calling him on the lies, and he could not have cared less.

Michael had no luck with his cell phones. I always found this strange, he would come home and say he lost his phone every 3 to 4 months. His IPod was another item that just seemed to disappear that we replaced often.

Our life together changed from a mutual loving respect to yelling matches, slamming doors, silence, and lies, and in the end, Michael would shut me out. Sometimes I would give in to him, just to have some decent time with my son. I held on to the lies, and I convinced myself that he was telling me the truth.

I spent hours, days, and years standing by the sidelines, with hope that he would return to me again, as I once knew him. Michael became my obsession and my addiction. I spent days in my own web of lies and denial. I protected him, I wanted no one to know, I gave in to him. I believed him when he lied. I justified it when he stole. I could not lose him. No matter who he was and who he had become he was my son and I loved him.

The death of my son is a pain so deep that it cannot be expressed into words, and everyone experiences it in their own way. I was faced with emotions that I believed would never exist in my being. I felt like I was drowning. I felt I was paralyzed, nothing felt real. Everything became jaded. What is happening to me? I would wonder. Did I care? No! I just wanted to run, be alone, and the possibility of dying was always there. I decided to talk to other parents who have also lost a child. It was helpful, because they share a similar pain experience, but even between grieving parents the mourning process can vary greatly. It is not uncommon for grieving parents to distance themselves from old friends or family members, I know this was true for me.

The death of a child is life-changing. I am not the same person that I was before Michael's death. Early in my grief journey I was disoriented because the sense of how my life with Michael would play out had been destroyed. As I picked up the pieces of my broken life, I discovered new strengths and build a new set of beliefs to live by. I found myself driven by a conviction that I must make the most of the time I have, because I realized that life is too short.

My grief will never cease to exist, but at some point the grief will not consume my life as wholly as it did in the beginning. I started setting new habits, rituals, and traditions to remember the joy that Michael brought into our life, this has helped me in keeping Michael's memory alive.

The death of my son has given me the opportunity to return to love and faith in God. The belief in the afterlife has eased my mind in knowing that Michael and I are, and always be, sharing Eternal Love.

My life without my son will never be the same. I will take the risk of believing and see where it leads me. I will not be intimidated by the opinions of others on how I should be feeling. I know Michael is with me always as I am with him. My faith is found in my unconditional love for Michael, and not in the degree of my grieving. Most importantly I will not be afraid. As Michael said, "when you are afraid... you are not living!"

Every day our kids have to make choices that we, as parents, never even dreamed about when we were kids. Peer pressure is a powerful thing, and many times, our kids will reluctantly go along with the crowd and do things that they are not comfortable with and know are harmful in order to gain acceptance.

The pressure to belong and fit in is widespread an unrelenting. Yet despite this, we have come into this life to experience freedom. From an early age, schools, our families and cultural influences push us to follow certain behaviors, norms and rules. For some of us, the feeling of belonging is comforting and provides a sense of identity, friendship and connection to others. But sometimes the expectations of others can also create inner turmoil, tension and confusion.

This behavior repeated itself with Michael and over time it manifested itself in a full-blown drug addiction and ultimately, his death. As parents, how can we tell if our children are abusing substances? This was a question I asked myself 24-hours a day. Do I want to know? Maybe it's just a phase? He's experimenting... and so on. Unfortunately, too many parents really don't want to know the answer, I certainly did not, because this is one subject that was too scary, frustrating and guilt-laden to deal with.

As it is very difficult for me to address some of these symptoms, I realize that I am addressing the Michael I did not know, the symptoms of his disease. And for all of you parents experiencing this or have experienced it, please know that you are not alone. I thought I was. I did not want anyone to find out The shame of it all. The last four years of Michael's life were relentless. There were times I did not know if he was going to make it. I only know, that God does not give you more then you can handle.

These are some of the signs Michael demonstrated. There are many more out there, I am only listing what I have experienced. I encourage you to look further if you are experiencing this disease as a parent.

My loving Michael turned mean, angry and aggressive. This happened with the onset of puberty for Michael, but it is much worse when there is substance abuse going on. No matter what I said or did, I could just not win! I was afraid or reluctant to confront my child due to violent outbursts or reactions from him when I attempted to inquire about any part of his life. Just remember, when a kid is backed into a corner, he may have discovered that the best defence is an offense. Many teens, particularly boys, find that by coming back with loud yelling, they can be very intimidating to their mothers. I am proof of this act. I feared my own son. Suspect drug use if your child has lately become very irritable, unpleasant, or is bullying other family members, if he is very easy to provoke, starts to use a lot of profanity, seems tired, worn out, sleeps most of the day away and is apathetic a lot of the time, or develops a nagging cough, has constants sniffles, runny nose, or nosebleeds.

His appearance went down the tubes. Michael was always a sharp dressed young man. Only the best brand of clothing hung in his closet. I started wondering why he did not care about his appearance anymore. He wore track pants that were too baggy on him, and t-shirts with negative or drug sayings on them. These kind of clothes may attract other kids who use drugs, and cause kids who are not into that scene to shy away from your child.

Michael stopped looking after his personal hygiene, and did not care about his looks any longer. His clothes smelled like marijuana, his hair was not washed and stringy. He used profanity to get me off his back when I pointed it out to him. His favorite saying to me was, "What the fuck, mom, relax!" He wore dark sunglasses all the time. His eyes where red and he was never out of Visine eye drops. And most of all, it was heart breaking to stand there on the sidelines and watch him lose his passion and zest for life.

Michael never ever admitted who some of his friends were who abused drugs. He kept this a "secret" along with protecting his cell phone. He would always have me drop him off to a friend's house who I knew. His whereabouts after that would remain a mystery. If you really think that drug-using friends are considerate enough not to do drugs in front of your child or that your child is just sitting around watching them use while not using himself, think again. If your child is actually resisting taking the drugs, you can be sure he is being goaded and coaxed into using along with the friends. Misery loves company, and it's no fun to get high by yourself. Kids who are not using do not pick users as friends. It is also no fun to sit around and watch other people get "stupid" on you. So you can bet that if your child's friends are using drugs, then he/she is using with them.

I remember one Saturday morning Michael coming out of the shower and walked out of the bathroom with just a towel wrapped around his waist. I took a double-take, I could not believe my eyes. I could count his ribs and his shoulder joints and collar bone were pronating out of his skin. I questioned what was going on and he assured me that he was watching his weight. I really believed him, because as a young boy he was overweight and had issues with his weight throughout his childhood and early adolescence. So I immediately backed off the subject. But I went on about the fact that he had gone too far and he should start eating and just make better choices with food. For Michael, it was a cover up for the abuse of methamphetamines, which speed up the system and took away his appetite, thereby causing drastic changes in his weight.

Michael came home and cleaned out the pantry. This was also a sign that Michael had just been out smoking pot, which is notorious for causing "the munchies." I would find countless boxes of cookies, chips and crackers underneath his bed when I searched his room.

This behavior was accompanied by red eyes, slurred speech, nasty temper, uncontrollable laughing or exceptional drowsiness, I was sure that Michael had been up to something. Also, he did not smell pretty. Pot smell is very prominent, it gets everywhere including his hair and clothes. Parents and caregivers please keep in mind that the marijuana our kids get hold of today is many times stronger than the pot that was available when many of today's parents were kids, and it is far more harmful. It is now often laced with other drugs. Marijuana can cause permanent short-term memory loss, particularly in younger kids whose brains are still developing. Marijuana is in no way a "harmless drug" as many of its proponents would like us to believe. In my son Michael's case it was the gateway drug that lead him to his death.

No one sets out to become an addict. What are children are searching for is the escape from dulling the pain that often comes with the ups and downs of everyday life. Every day this world announces illusionary and deafening ways to find bliss and yes, this includes our children and drugs.

Michael's sole preoccupation was getting a hold of enough money to fund his habit and he soon started stealing to fund his lifestyle. Money, jewelry, PlayStation, Xbox, all went missing from our home. Every three to four months or so, he would say that he lost his cell phone. It was only later that we realized these things had been sold for drugs.

After all the signs and symptoms of my son's addiction. I still could not face the reality that was in front of me. I just wanted to keep my head under the covers and when I emerged, everything would be back to normal and Michael and I could resume our loving relationship.

Michael's death left me with a trail of emotional upheaval, numbness and despair. When Michael died I thought I lost my life. I didn't know where to turn for answers. After all, I was raised Catholic. This belief limited me and made it difficult for me to ask questions. Nevertheless, my mind could not rest. The only thoughts I would have constantly were: Where are you Michael? Are you safe? Are you alone? Are you homesick? Why did you leave me? I had to find my son!

During all my despair and deep grief and my broken heart, Michael did his best to leave signs for me to let me know that he did not leave me and he is with me always.

I would hear "I am not dead mom!" I finally fell asleep for a few hours before the planning of his funeral, and I asked him, Please Michael, where are you? In my dream state, Michael appears in a Golden Meadow with his soccer ball, his six-year-old self. He is dressed in his white t-shirt and black shorts, having fun kicking the ball around. He kicks the ball to me and says: "Run mommy, run, faster, get the ball, mommy!" Till this day, I hear him laughing so joyfully while he was playing with me in that Golden Meadow.

While planning his funeral, I felt like I was cut off from my feelings. I was observing this woman (me) going through the motions. I saw her pain and suffering but I was not connected to her. I had lost my identity.

I specifically remember walking through the funeral home trying to choose a casket. I would hear: "Mommy, I love this one... it has a lot of personality and great lines." I was standing right in front of the one I was marvelling." Me: How can you love a casket? The only thought I had was: Once you are in it, I can never hold you again. Michael's reply to me was: "I am holding you right now."

With all the pain and suffering, I dismissed all the never ending love from him, because I thought: This is not real, Michael you are coming home right?

Right after his funeral, Michael's attempts to get my attention were endless. He would move my jewelry around, from the dresser to the bed. He used the same bracelet all the time. The first time it happened, I just assumed that I had lost the bracelet. He kept on doing it until I paid attention. Other times I would be driving and I would feel his presence guiding me to this or that radio station, every time hearing songs with the same theme of messages of love and forgiveness. The first song he chose for me was "I Bet my Life", from Imagine Dragons.

Here are a few of the verses from this beautiful song:
I know I took the path that you would never want for me
I know I let you down, didn't I?
So many sleepless nights where you were waiting up on me
Well I'm just a slave unto the night
Now remember when I told you that's the last you'll see of me
Remember when I broke you down to tears
I know I took the path that you would never want for me
I gave you hell through all the years
I've been around the world and never in my wildest dreams
Would I come running home to you
I've told a million lies but now I tell a single truth
There's you in everything I do

Michael loved music. I believe it comes with his Artist abilities to express his feelings through music and art, but unfortunately he kept this expression to himself.

After his death I would walk out in the mornings and find a white rose or red rose by my car door. I would hear Michael when I was getting dressed, especially if he liked what I was wearing, I can hear his sweet voice saying "you look beautiful mom!" I would question these acts of love with Michael all the time. Am I going crazy? What is happening to me? The divine part of me would assure me that this real, Michael confirmed what I saw and heard was real: "Trust this mom!" "There is life after death, I am not dead!"

Michael's passing left a trail of various states of emotional upheaval. From the upheaval though came a great wonderful gift. A spiritual awakening that becomes stronger and richer every day. A week before Michael's death, his life was the worst I had ever seen. I prayed constantly for him, for me and for our family. As far as I was concerned, I was walking this path and life lesson alone. But I was certain that I had enough faith in God that He would not leave me. Then, Michael disappeared from home two days before his passing, and I was left in "hell." I retreated to my office, shut the door and I fell on my knees and I asked God the following: "Please Father of Heaven and Earth, help Michael, he is yours to do what is your will. Please think of Michael first, I place him in your loving heart and caring hands, please make him happy and healthy, and please return Michael to me whole, happy, healthy and safe. Amen." And He did!

God's Will was done. He answered my prayer, but I was not pleased with God. I was sent in a state of shock and pain filled with grief and I felt punished, to say the very least. WHY WOULD A LOVING GOD be so cruel as to take Michael away from me?

I trusted God; I refused to understand why God would do this to me, why Michael would do this to me. What I failed to understand was that He did, indeed, return Michael to me just as I asked, not in a physical state, but in a Holy state.

For many of us parents, the loss of our child also means another change. "Who am I without my child?" I felt incapable of living life without my Michael. I remember holding back my emotions and I did not want to express how I felt about Michael's death, but each day the overwhelming wave got worse like a snowball rolling down hill, picking up more snow, more momentum and speed as it rolls down. The first few months of my grief I often recall as the "robotic phase." I was numb, the significant role I had with Michael was gone.

We all have different belief systems, different levels of spiritual understanding, and once again we are faced with a choice; we can either grow stronger or be controlled by our circumstances and be paralyzed with fear. I personally chose to grow stronger. One of the first steps I took in my healing journey is to live the life that Michael would be proud of. I can continue to teach my child how to handle life situations in a positive way. I decided that I would turn this tragedy into service and create a positive outcome.

No matter how a child dies, whether from a freak accident, an overdose of drugs, or a terminal illness, the first sense he or she has when leaving the body is one of freedom. Think of it as taking off a heavy overcoat in the heat of a hot summer day. All the pain, torment and suffering are gone. The suffering, powerlessness, helplessness they once felt on earth quickly fades away. Instead, the spirit feels incredible joyfulness and an overwhelming sense of peace.

Michael's passing is an ending of one part of my life, but also the beginning of another. Once I was able to accept what happened to Michael, forgive myself and forgive Michael, I became someone who could help heal the world.

Acceptance and forgiveness allow us to start a new chapter in our lives and clear our space for new opportunities to reach us. Michael has given me a gift– and a new life purpose. It is up to me to fulfill my soul's purpose and mission in life.

One of the most challenging tests of love is our ability to let go. In the physical realm, we think love as being close to one another, holding hands, talking, looking into one another's eyes, sharing activities and cuddling. The call to experience a higher form of love often comes in the most difficult ways. When there is a committed love bond between two people on a soul level, the connection is extremely strong. This bond transcends the veil and goes beyond death of the human body.

Michael's death is the Great Awakener. When Michael passed over to Heaven, part of me went with him. Even when I know in my heart and in communicating with him every day that he is safe in Heaven among our family and friends, I still miss him. Grieving is a process that like death, shook me to the core. Compassion, understanding, and supportive family and friends help me through the difficult and lonely days and nights. But it is still not easy. When Michael passed on I experienced an emptiness that nothing seems to fill. I can truly say, his death made its way into my life. I am forever changed.

My deceased child does not want me to feel sad. He has on many occasions insisted that I move on with my life in the best possible way. The loss of Michael caused me to feel unbearable guilt, blame, doubt, fear, and anguish. No words are enough, no hugs and kisses are enough, nothing seems enough to console me. Grieving parents are different from others who are grieving. All expectations for a normal life are shattered for us. It has been the most painful experience imaginable for me and there is no quick fix. It takes time, love and effort to move forward. Patience above all, is essential.

Although, there is no set way for someone to grieve, I have learned that there are healthy ways to go through the process. One of the most valuable insights I can share is to remind you to attempt, as best as you can, to place yourself in a state of mindfulness. It is important not only to be aware of yourself as a spiritual, energetic being, but also to live that way every single day.

Healthy grief means dealing with emotions. Unhealthy grief means masking or numbing emotions. I have found through journal writing and letter writing, and meditation with Michael has helped me better understand life after death. I talk to Michael through meditation, prayer and automatic writing and in return it opens up my senses to receive messages in return from Michael.

Although I am grieving Michael's passing over, I realized that it is important to be aware that I am still and forever will be a source of love to him. When Michael's death arrived, he seemed forever gone. But he is not. Yet communicating and connecting with him, not only helps me, but also supports him in many ways.

Michael's gift to me, and what makes me happy, and where I most succeed, is in the love that engages my spirit. I have accepted that I am right where I am meant to be, doing exactly at this time what I am meant to do right in this moment.

I believe love will conquer all. Once we get to the realization of loving ourselves and breathing that love into every single experience of every single day, then you start to make a big progression at that point. There are no strings attached to love. Love does not hold back. As we are made in the likeness of God and God is Love, then we must strive to express our love in everyone and in everything we do, say and are. There is no separation in the Love of God.

Love yourself unconditionally. Take time for you. Understand you. Honor whatever emotion comes up, it is okay, to love even those unwanted thoughts and emotions, that is what the moment is asking you to do. We are made of God's loving energy. Recognize it; enjoy it; and forgive yourself. Our loved ones are not in pain anymore... they are freed.

This story is dedicated in memory of my son,
Michael Anthony
(June 10th, 1996 – March 11th, 2015)

My precious Michael, my heart, thank you for your endless love... you transformed death into life and made it something beautiful. You have shared your love with me and others and you are guiding and helping me and others all over the world. I am so very proud of you! No words could ever describe my love for you. I miss you, I miss the hugs and kisses, I miss our "date nights." I miss telling you to be good and be careful when you were leaving for school or going out with your friends. I still have some tough days with grief, but I am happy for you, I really am. Michael, I never want this to go unsaid.

There are no words to express how much you mean to me. The day you were born, God sent me a blessing— and that was you. For this I thank Him every day. You are the true definition of a son, in every way. It is because of you that my life has meaning. Always remember that I know how much you love me and how much you care, I can tell by the relationship that we share. Whether we are together or apart, please do not ever forget— You will always have a piece of my heart!

I love you, forever my heart, Momma.

Tina Aurelio is a highly motivated "wellnesspreneur", life coach, and motivational speaker, dedicated to empowering individuals. Tina educates on a holistic approach to designing an optimal lifestyle. She demonstrates focus to a life of vitality and connected purpose. Today, she combines her knowledge and experience about the physical, emotional and spiritual body to help individuals connect to the core vitality that spurs truly remarkable lives.

Tina's life purpose is about inspiring, teaching and coaching individuals to achieve their best life. Tina draws on the lessons she's learned from her experiences to motivate people fulfill their potential.

I believe in implementing effective guidelines to create success and enable people to live life on their terms, healthy in mind, body and spirit."
~Tina Aurelio

Darcie Boland

My Search for Happiness

We are all born with the power to live our own lives and when we fall victim to someone else's needs, someone else's agenda, we lose ourselves. There is always a choice— go left... go right... stay... go, but why must I choose someone else's choice? Why have I based every single decision on what everyone else thinks? When did I give up my power? With that said, I don't think I really ever knew myself. I think I lost my power to make any decisions right from the moment I was born.

My mother was a teenager when she had me, and married my father. All I heard from a very young age was that, I should not make the same mistake. Mistake? I heard that many times growing up, so what was the mistake? MISTAKE is a big word for a child, and I feared making mistakes each and every day. Therefore, I only made decisions that would please everyone.

As a child, we moved around frequently to different areas of the city because of my father's job. Each move meant a different neighborhood and school. It was survival of the fittest as I had to make new friends every few years. Don't get me wrong, I loved meeting new people. I just didn't get that growing up together bond with any of my girlfriends. I'm grateful I have many friends throughout each phase of my life, and literally when a certain song comes on the radio I can picture exactly where and with whom I was with when the song was originally released. Growing up, I guess I was an average child, didn't mind school, enjoyed sports and kept my secrets to myself.

There was a lot of chaos at home— a lot of yelling, screaming, fighting, and drinking. Looking back now, I realize that my parents were so young that they were just victims as well. I never felt that I truly belonged anywhere, not wanting anymore fighting and yelling, so, I kept silent about the years of sexual molestation I had endured, away from my parents– I never told anyone. I truly believed it was my fault, that I was dirty and I should be punished. I did not want anyone to dislike me, I craved for approval, attention, love, and quietness. I always thought I was to blame for my parents conflicts all the time, since I figured out I was the mistake.

A few months before I was about to start high school, we moved yet again, only this time, it was a big move to a small town. It was one of the hardest times for me and I'm sure my parents too. Relocating a teenage daughter with no self–love, arming herself with a full-set of adolescent armor willing to attack. I thought my parents fought, but boy, oh boy, did my mom and I go at it for the four years of high school. I was lost, I can remember trying to fit in every single day. I would say what you wanted me to say, I would do what you wanted me to do, as long as you liked me. I had no idea who I was, or what I was going to do with my life? I did know that I was going to travel all around the world where I can be free and happy. Little did I know that happiness comes from within.

When I was younger, I would sometimes stay at my great-grandmother's and on Friday nights she would let me stay up and watch The Love Boat and Fantasy Island. 'That was it,' I thought to myself. 'I'm going to work on The Love Boat!' So, all through high school I just coasted by, because I was going to leave and travel the world. Unfortunately, I still needed to get through the four years. I made a few friends but it was difficult, as I just couldn't fit in, was teased and made fun of a lot by the other kids. Sometimes my "friends" would just decide they didn't want to talk to me anymore, and I had to go and find new friends. At least I had the previous experience of making new friends, so I just did. Looking back at it now, it seemed harsh but then again, I never had any boundaries, I really didn't know how I should be treated. Even on my daily bus ride, to and from school was humiliating, the boys would lift my kilt and laugh, saying I had skid marks, EVERY single day. When you're so used to being victimized, your perception of what's right and wrong is no longer valid. It's like you're a magnet to this kind of behavior. My father used to tell me, "you have a black cloud over you."

This low self-esteem continued, as I even lost my virginity to a date rape, because he didn't think that I really meant "NO." I still remember asking him, "it didn't happen, right?" He told me to look down at the sheet. As I gathered up the bloodstained sheet and put it in my bag, a single tear fell from my face and I never spoke a word to anyone about that night. The thing with keeping so many secrets is that, sometimes, you need to lie to keep them, and in doing so, I became unintentionally, a very good liar. A year later, I dated another guy who I convinced, he was my first, so I had a better and more normal story to share with my girlfriends about "the first time."

As I continued with the stories the more I felt alone. I needed to go far away, I did not know what I was looking for, but that feeling was so strong it was pulling me. I just knew that happiness was around the corner. It had to be. I sent out a few hundred resumes, snail mail back in the day. It seemed that the only responses I received was the old "thank you for your interest with...." but then one day it happened, I got the call that changed my life forever.

Three weeks later I was down in Miami and about to take my first ship out of wet dock and reposition it to Aruba to be my homeport for the next eight months. Wow! It was so amazing, and so surreal. I was so young and naïve that I was still projecting many insecurities which allowed me to fall victim to the most humiliating prank that one can actually pull off. I was put in charge of "Dolphin watch", clearly, I believed "Him", after all he was my casino manager. I didn't want to ever do anything wrong and I always did what I was told. I was told to dress smart and collect the clip board, binoculars and radio and report to the very bow (front) of the ship. I did just that. The wind was blowing so hard and I was upset with myself for being an idiot to wear a skirt because I only had two hands, one to hold the clip board and the other to hold the radio-binoculars where around my neck which meant every few seconds the skirt flew up. I was starting to lose my patience with Greenpeace because there's no possible way I can see a bloody dolphin in this wind! Finally, I got a message on the radio asking if I see anything. I said I'm having trouble in this wind, are you sure I'm supposed to be here? Don't you think the dolphin will see us before I see him? My manager said, just a little longer or something along those words and I continued with my "Dolphin Watch." About 20 minutes later I got another message on the radio saying I can come in now. Thank God, I said to myself as I turned around to go back inside. Just then, in that very moment the same wave of humiliation rushed through me, the one I knew so well. I was standing there staring at a couple of hundred crew members laughing at me and as I looked up I saw all the officers on the bridge as well, watching. Mortified, I ran back to my cabin. I'm not even sure what happened over the next few days, I just did my duties until we arrived in the port of Aruba. It's amazing how I internalized it and never said a word. I mean I chuckled a bit when I was asked about it, pretending it didn't bother me. What bothered me was me, why did they pick me? What's wrong with me? Why am I such a loser? None the less, I was scarred for life and vowed never to be a part of any initiation ritual.

Looking back on my career in the cruise lines, I never was alone— I always had a boyfriend. I didn't even realize that I couldn't be alone. I had no idea who I was, and that I depended on them to make me happy. Once we got bored of each other I moved on. I'm sure I must have drove them crazy because I was so insecure and needy. I became the perfect girlfriend— always wanting to do what they wanted to do, to the point that I would resent them and start acting crazy. This went on for 9 years, the same exact pattern just a different name. I didn't know what a healthy relationship was, I just thought I didn't want to be alone. My parents were not an example of a healthy, loving couple. In fact, quite the opposite. I do know, however, that my mother always said she couldn't leave because of the kids and never wanted to live alone. So, she would do everything to make things work. She did. There wasn't anything she wouldn't do for her family. I do believe that we develop learned behavior patterns from our parents and they, theirs. I know that I became very codependent and it kept me from knowing myself, loving myself and having boundaries in all my relationships.

In my last year of working on the cruise ships, I met a man who eventually became my husband and the father of my beautiful and amazing son and daughter. Unfortunately, my past behavior patterns caught up with me and just because you have children and a piece of paper doesn't mean it's meant to be. I felt more alone than ever. I mean I loved and adored my children, but I couldn't stop crying. I cried myself to sleep every night. I still remember being told "you're never happy!" I wasn't happy. I was still searching for it, still longing for something to fill this void that I've carried around all my life. This went on for years and I'm not even sure how I was able to leave my marriage because I knew with every fiber of my being I needed to make this work and not be a single mother.

I was living a secret, I was lying to myself and most of all, I was teaching my children the same thing. The exact learned behaviors that have been passed down from two generations that I know of, I was repeating. I was in a battle constantly with myself, should I end this or not? The only words I heard running through my head were my mother's over and over again – "don't leave if you're going to change your mind, make sure you make the right decision." Those words weighed heavily on me, and how I found the strength to go against them is a miracle in its self. I believe that the men I attracted in my life including my now ex-husband, were influenced by the male role models I had growing up. I had no self-respect, no boundaries, wanted no conflict and kept my mouth shut. I was searching for validation and felt completely unlovable.

Still looking on the outside, still searching for "true happiness." Just because I made a geographical change, my codependency was still in full force and I was living on my own with my children. Insecurity, vulnerability, you name it, I oozed these. I was sending out the wrong frequency and definitely attracting the wrong men. One day I met a man. I thought things had changed and it would be different. We dated for eighteen months. It was fun and I truly believed we knew each other. He had one daughter and we all got along really well. The five of us went everywhere and it felt like a family and I thought, "ok, this will work out." "I can do this," it wasn't about me. It was about my children and their happiness. I've kept secrets all my life, I just needed my children to be happy.

I remember the day we moved into his house, believe me, he always made it clear it was his house. I was so sick to my stomach, I couldn't sleep and so this was where I ended up again. Making it work! The red flags were there. Looking back, there had always been signs for me, but I lacked confidence and more importantly I did not trust myself. How could I? I never knew who I was or what I wanted. I was on a quest to find happiness through someone else.

The first week we were there, he let go of the maid, I guess that's my job now. He knew that I had my children all the time and he had his daughter every other week. To this extent, on the weeks he didn't have his daughter it was a living nightmare. I felt like I was walking on egg shells making sure my children didn't upset him, which everything set him off! It was as if I never met this person, I dated him for eighteen months! Who is this man I'm living with? He had told me many lies about his past - through omission of important information. When I would confront him about them, he would remind me that I should be grateful that my children and myself are able to live in a house like this. Every day became a struggle, and I just kept telling myself, "I can do this for three more years until both my children are off to university and I can leave." Before we moved in, we made arrangements that I would pay rent and 1/3 of the household bills. I would receive a monthly invoice of the bills that needed to be paid. After a couple of months, he decided that I should pay $1/2$ of the household bills since my children were there more. My income had not changed, my children were still with me the same amount of time as before. I had moved in with a controlling narcissist, how do I make this work? He even bought his daughter's and his own groceries and would label them with their initials because we weren't allowed to eat his food. I made the mistake once, making one of his frozen pizzas and had a strip torn off me. To this day I don't eat frozen pizza. He grew angrier and angrier, probably because I wasn't as much fun to be around anymore. I didn't do anything, with limited friends and no interests, by no choice of mine. I was just buying time. I could tell he wanted us out, because money was a constant issue— he had millions and I had debt. The solution, he said, was for me to get a real career that paid for this kind of lifestyle. He stated that I should be ashamed of myself for having two children and not being able to take care of them. I was doing the exact same thing as I was doing when he met me and he knew the income I was making. I did feel ashamed, I did feel guilty, I was so embarrassed and humiliated, that I didn't tell a soul how I was being treated. But, the familiarity of all those feelings of not being worthy, not being deserving and not being lovable was all that I knew and I should be able to make this work. It was as if this behavior was normal to me and I need to focus on my children and do whatever it takes. I did not want to end up alone and disappoint my family.

I must have missed that email, find new career! That's how he communicated, he would send me an email whenever we had to discuss something. This was a whopper of a secret, I was dying inside and I couldn't tell anyone because I didn't know how to. I did not know how to tell someone how I was feeling, ask for help or even know that I deserve to be treated better. Again, I thought this was my fault because all I kept hearing was my mother's voice. She told me when I decided to move into his place, "if you move in, whatever you do don't fuck up my grandchildren."

There was no way I was going to fail again, I allowed myself to be prisoner and bullied for twenty-two months. One day the stress became unbearable, I collapsed at work and was taken to the hospital in an ambulance and all I could think of was what will my family think of me? How can I be such a failure? Why does this keep happening to me? How am I going to take care of my children alone? Up until the hospital incident, I was still considering making it work just for a few more years, but his narcissistic behavior was no longer just directed at me. He started to take it out on my children and I guess I couldn't deal with that. I needed to protect them and with every ounce of strength I could muster up, I asked for help and moved us out in a day. My mother and brother where right there helping us and from that day on they've been so supportive that words cannot describe enough how grateful I am to have them as my family.

I know that all of these events happened because this was my journey. This was a lesson I needed in self-love, if I didn't get it this time who knows where I would be? I started the work, I started the long haul of taking back my power and my ownership of my life. It was scary. I had a personal training job which I loved, but it wasn't keeping us afloat and being so far in debt it was hard to pay the interest and monthly rent and bills. I really thought long and hard about the next phase of my life. I thought about how I got to where I am, and how I was going to change. How was I going to love myself? Everything I was learning and working on always came back to loving and approving of yourself. I realized that nothing I do or accomplish will ever make me happy if these two things don't happen.

For the first time in 45 years I started to have a relationship with myself. Slowly I began the process, it's not easy. It's a constant battle with my old default programing, I never realized how negatively I talked to myself. I had to do an exercise, I had to journal when I would say something negative to myself. My most common thoughts were, I'm stupid, I'm an idiot, what a loser, you look terrible today, better exercise more, think twice before you eat that, are you sure? What if you're wrong? Basically, I was constantly writing things down, to the point I actually would get mad at myself for being so mean to myself. That's when I realized I was starting to care about me.

I would wake up every morning early and do my positive affirmations and prayers. I am honest when I say this, but there's no way I believed any of those affirmations in the beginning but I just kept saying them because I was desperate to change and more importantly willing to change. As my self-esteem built up, so did my dreams. I was beginning to feel as though life wasn't over for me and that I can still have it all. I wanted to have that new career at middle age, I wanted to travel the world and write stories. I put out my resume and began my search within the airline industry. Things really do have a funny way of working out, when I said I wanted to work on the cruise ships I did, but I also wanted to be a flight attendant as well. I spent almost a year working on my French language because the industry has changed, a second language is no longer considered an asset but is required. I applied for a full-time bilingual flight attendant position and have now earned my wings.

This process or change however you want to call it, takes a lot of hard work and honesty. Complete honesty is the most humbling experience. I may have been a victim when I was a child, but that isn't who I am today. Since I couldn't get out of that "I'm a survivor" mentality, I was still stuck as being a victim. If you're a survivor, that means you were a victim. I needed to let go of my past and all past experiences and detach myself from being a victim.

Since I whole heartedly love and approve of myself today, my life has changed drastically. Many new women have come into my life. Every single day, I am so blessed to share with them my experience, strength and hope. I've been so lucky to have a second chance, or a first chance for that matter, to get to know myself and to smile beyond belief, that I, by the grace of God am perfect exactly the way I am. I was born to be me and the search for happiness has always lived inside of me.

Finding the strength through faith and gratitude I have a new story to write. A single mother of two teenagers soon to embark on their own journey, I prayed for the "courage to change the things I can." Mid-life and a one hundred and eighty degree change I find myself for the first time in my life. I refuse to go down in fear and negativity. I believe I am supported in my faith and my spiritual connection, I believe in myself and I am without a doubt, Born to be me.

Angela Catenaro McNeill

Diary of a Recovering People Pleaser

I woke up with the thought– hmmm I am getting married today. Just a thought. No excitement, no joy. Just a thought. I was 21 years old (just two months shy of my 22nd birthday) and getting married to my high school sweetheart. I didn't have the awareness at the time that I wasn't happy– 'ya woulda thunk' that the lack of excitement could have been an AHA moment– but it wasn't, I needed a smack on my butt to finally wake up. Thank God I did. It just took 3 more years.

Something was missing from my life. What? Me. The real me. I had dated Aaron for 7 years on and off until he proposed. As I write this, I still feel the sadness for the scared little girl I was. I started dating Aaron when I was 15, the nice girl who desperately wanted to fit in and be liked. The lingering feeling that I was different than others made me want to be a part of the group and just fit in. Often teased for my sensitivity, my natural empathy and helpfulness made me the easy target of the "bully personality."

Aaron asked me out as the school year of grade eleven started. I hadn't dated much and he was a popular guy in school, so I said yes. After two weeks of dating, I really wasn't into him and was about to break up with him when he said the magic words "I love you." BAM! I was hooked. How could I abandon someone who loved me? Little insignificant me was loved by him!

Aaron became my whole world. I lost friends and gained friends while I was with him. My adolescent years in finding my own identity was a steady metamorphosis into a girl who was a "people pleaser" and doormat.

A shift in this evolution came about a year into our relationship, Aaron broke up with me. The words "I don't love you anymore" crushing my chest like an elephant sitting on me. There was another girl. I didn't know what to do with myself. The hurt and insecurity was unbearable. After two weeks of being apart, Aaron called me vowing that he loved and missed me, he had made a mistake and can't live without me. We got back together.

This became the pattern in our relationship. Every year or so, he'd break off with me, same line— I don't love you anymore blah blah blah. Wait two three weeks, he'd call me, I love you, miss you, can't live without you, blah blah blah. The part of it all that makes my insides melt with sadness is, I always welcomed him back into my life every time.

Even as I write this, the feelings of shame wash over me— not to the same intensity as some time ago, but nonetheless, the shame is still present. I love that little scared insecure people-pleasing lost girl. I feel so sorry for the decisions that I made while I was her but she didn't know better. I was young and naïve believing that love hurt and that when you loved someone you took the good, the bad, and the ugly. I naturally dismissed my intuitive senses because my worth was tied into his affection and validation. I hadn't been taught self-love, nor was I equipped with self-respect... these were the lessons I needed to learn in order to rise to find the real me.

I lost my virginity to Aaron. No pressure, it just happened naturally, we both wanted to because we were in love, right?

How this act was a huge catalyst to the girl I had become was the intensity of that love attention perpetuated and it left me feeling needy of Aaron's attention and affection. I convinced myself there was no other guy for me, we were soul mates – the intensity was so great that I'd give anything up to be with him.

When Aaron asked me to marry him, I affirmed "I will be the best wife to you." I never questioned if I loved him. I never questioned if he really loved me. All the intuitive red flags I tucked deep away in the big hope chest of denial. He was what I knew, and marrying him was what I believed the right thing to do. I had an idealistic view that our love would concur all, just like the Eagles' ballad, "When we are hungry, love will keep us alive." I was unconscious to the sadness, resentment, and unhappiness buried deep within me.

Fast forward two years, I was putting on my make up getting ready to go out for dinner to celebrate our 2-year anniversary when a feeling of heat in my gut and foreboding washed over me. I clearly felt something was going to happen. I stared at myself in the mirror and asked "Who are you?" I looked into my eyes and knew this was the beginning of the end.

Two months later, we took a trip to Mexico, along with a group of friends. As we planned an excursion, I wanted to go horseback riding, but all the guys wanted to go on a tour on an ATV. I didn't want to. I felt so much fear. I expressed I didn't want to go, but was told not be a deadbeat. Again, dismissing my intrinsic right to choose not to participate, I gave in to please him.

We had done a mini test on the ATV. A test pad made of hilly sand. I thought to myself, "okay, I can do this."

However, while we were riding into the forest, I fell off the ATV. Not too bad, but the tour guide asked if I would rather ride with my husband, so I left the ATV and rode with Aaron the rest of the way to the rest stop.

We stopped for lunch by the ocean. The tour guide told me that I had to ride the ATV back as they could not leave it there. I felt uneasy, but got back on it. We were riding up a mountain that had thick ridges made from water erosion. I struggled, while Aaron and the rest of the group were ahead of me. As I reached the top of the mountain the front tire got stuck within a ridge and I could not turn the steering away from the edge of the mountain. I could not stop. I was riding over the edge realizing OMG I am going to die– And I WAS OKAY WITH IT! What?

The ATV fell deep into the forest below while I hung to some weeds and branches on the edge of the mountain. At that moment I felt like I was resting on an invisible canopy, with a deep knowing that I was being held by loving forces that I could not see with my eyes– I just knew Angels held me.

People stopped to help and who came to my rescue was not my husband, but rather a friend. I hurt my shoulder and was in shock with thankfully no other injuries. I was driven to a local hospital where Aaron met me. He seemed concerned and protective of the doctor's care, yet I could feel something was lacking. The care he was expressing did not feel authentic. All I could think was I ruined the tour with my accident.

Even though I was feeling the disconnect months before, I felt our trip to Mexico was the catalyst to fracturing the rose colored glasses I was viewing my world with. Aaron became more distant and arrogant. I was beginning to dislike who Aaron was becoming (or realizing who he really was) and wondered secretly if I really loved him. My mind convinced me that this was just a phase. Again the feeling of unhappiness was my normal, so what could be wrong? Within two months, the old pattern resurfaced and Aaron finally told me that he no longer loved me; he felt that we had nothing in common. He wasn't wrong. He was right - we didn't have anything in common. The recognition hit that I didn't know myself. I didn't know what I liked, what I didn't like. I had been too fixated on being the person I thought Aaron wanted me to be that I completely lost myself to only again be rejected by him. How could Aaron love me when I didn't love myself? How could he know me, if I didn't know who I was? In living my life in fear of losing Aaron's conditional love, I lost my inner compass. We tried for a week or so to pretend that we could work it out until Aaron pushed me too far.

It was a Saturday night. I declined my friends' offer to go to the movies choosing to stay home with Aaron because we were working things out. Aaron's mood was dark and antagonistic. We sat down to dinner - I still remember with perfect clarity his look of loathing directed at me. We talked about taking a vacation and he said he wanted to go to Las Vegas ALONE; with a tone of contempt he accentuated the word ALONE. His words hit me... he had no intention of working it out with me; he has playing me like a fool as he had done so many other times before. The force of reality struck me in the gut and rage spilled out of me. I had to get away from him, but the more I moved away from him, the closer he came. I told him to stay away as I felt out of control. Of course, he didn't listen to me, he never did. His words taunting me, his body language navigating me in the direction to give him the perfect reason to leave. He wanted to be let off the hook and that is exactly what I did. As Aaron reached for me, I pushed my hand out and hit him in the mouth. He stumbled back, calling me a bitch. I shouted for him to get out. He put some clothes into a bag and left.

I can still feel how good it felt to push him away and kick him out of my house! The years of swallowing feelings of anger and resentment burst to the surface because I finally had enough of being played like a puppet. Yet, the euphoria of kicking him out didn't last long. The shame of losing control and giving him the reason to blame me was crippling. He was right. I acted crazy. To this day, Aaron has been the only person who could bring out the worst side of me. He knew all my buttons and gladly pushed them at will.

For a couple of months following, my awareness danced between the illusion of "our love will concur all" to the reality of the lie I had been living.

During this time, I prayed for Aaron to come back, all the while I started to open up to the realization that I didn't even know why I loved him. I was in love with the notion of being in love. I really did not love Aaron. I didn't like him most of the time, so how could I love him? I was finally ready to see the type of love Aaron and I shared; it was conditional, immature and infatuating. I am not sure why he married me, but I realized why I married him. It was the type of love that felt like "home." Not the warm, nurturing, safe home, but the home filled with obstacle 'booby traps' that you would have to maneuver with all your might to avoid getting trapped. I was raised to believe that a good life was to find a job, get married, have kids. The only way to start a life of my own was to get married, and

I thought Aaron was my escape. While all-a-long, he was really my cage that I had constructed.

This kept me asleep and away from raising my consciousness to the reality of self-respect. I married Aaron because that was what I thought I deserved to experience. The illusion was I believed that getting married would give me the escape to create my own life of safety, security, and freedom. The irony was the fact I was not free. I was chained by own limiting beliefs of who a good girl was and what a good girl did.

I romanticized my relationship with Aaron because I was too afraid to go through life alone. Being with him made me feel cozy, like the feeling you get when you wrap yourself in a warm fuzzy blanket on a cold winter's day. Any time my intuitive self would try to raise my awareness, I would shut it down. I didn't want to wake up because I was petrified that I would fall apart. I wrapped my identity of who I was, with what he thought I was, who my family and friends told me I was, what society said was good or bad. If I took the security blanket of what I perceived love to be, then who was I? What kept me in a toxic relationship for so long was the fear of facing my fractured self.

I realized I was living a life that I bought into, but it was actually someone else's version of happy. That girl, was so afraid if she didn't play nice, her whole existence would fall apart. This life was not for her and the universe had to break her wide open to wake up.

At that time in my life, I was not able to be my true self, not only with Aaron but with the majority of the people that I surrounded myself with. When someone asked me how I was, my response was always "fine, how are you?" I always deflected any attention to my well-being back onto another person. I wore the mask of the good, dependable girl that was eternally grateful when someone noticed me.

Through the process of forgiveness, I had to ask myself, why didn't I run the very first time he broke up with me to go out with that girl from the billiards? Okay not then, but why didn't I hit the road for few years later when he slept with that stripper? Okay not then, well it could have been the time he asked to get back with me and my whole body was screaming NO!? Nope! Wasn't ready! Actually, my healing process of forgiveness wasn't for the act of marrying Aaron, it was for the years of self-betrayal.

Why did I continually betray myself by remaining in a relationship that wasn't healthy? At the time, I didn't know that the relationship was toxic but through this healing journey I have learned that Aaron's personality was what I already knew, what was familiar to me. The familiarity of Aaron's personality made me feel like I could handle it. It brought feelings of certainty and safety. I was putting a Band-Aid on my small child's heart who craved a stable, loving relationship; thinking that if I could start a life of my own then I would feel more in control of my life. The reality was, however, I had just been reliving patterns that maintained the feelings of unworthiness and lack of love.

Dismissing my intuitive senses, I had convinced myself that our differences made for a perfect partnership. I thought I balanced him and grounded him. I thought I could fix him and he would change to be better. Notice the common thread - HIM. I focused all my attention on his needs and wants.

I had buried my authentic self so deep in the illusion of external validation in order to feel accepted and loved by being in a stable, secure relationship. However, in actual reality, I was not in a safe or stable relationship. I was repeatedly unaccepted and loved conditionally. I didn't FEEL worthy to be loved and accepted. HE didn't need fixing – I DID! And thank GOD, the universe had my back.

I finally woke up and reached for the lifesaver. The universe knew I was living a lie. I was living a life meant for someone else, not me. I was going through the unconscious motion of being the good girl, doing the "right" things in life to be happy, while all along spinning my wheels digging myself deeper away from my authentic self.

What woke me up was the counsel from a priest - YES you read it right - a priest's guidance triggered my AHA moment!!! As I shared my despair of the situation, he said to me, "Why do you want a man who doesn't want you?" What? "Call a lawyer and change the locks to your house. This man is sick in the head." What? I too can make the choice to walk away. What? I don't have to suffer? Thank you GOD! This time I listened! I called a lawyer and changed the locks on the doors.

An inspiration hit me as Aaron and I had to go together to remove my name of documentation on his vehicle. As I was sitting in the passenger seat doing my best to look like "I'm okay", Matchbox Twenty's song Push sang out on the radio. For the 1st time I heard this song, it spoke to me. The lyrics told me how I was feeling at a time when I didn't know. That was a huge revelation for me. I felt manipulated and taken advantage of and I allowed it all. This feeling was so part of our relationship that I didn't even know that what I had experienced was abuse. It was always about Aaron's feelings, what he wanted, what he liked. I didn't know who I was because I spent so much time trying to be the person I thought he wanted; losing myself in order to be loved by him. In the end, my self-betrayal didn't make him love me. He still rejected me with a cold vengeance that told me I wasn't good enough and that he hated my personality. Of course he did! I was so unhappy and a doormat! How could he love me; I was not giving myself the love I desperately wanted to feel from him. I had taught him to "push" me around. I showed him that I was weak and sad (in truth my authentic self has an inner strength and trust that encourages me to get back up every time). I believed what others said about me and being the nice person meant you turned the other cheek and gave 150% to those you loved.

Rob Thomas' lyrics were liberating; allowing the feelings of anger, disappointment, and regret to bubble to the surface. Getting lost in the music gave me an outlet; helped me tap into my inner strength and realize that I am worth it, even though the person who promised to love me forever said I wasn't. He didn't matter anymore, I did NOW!

I thought I needed him to love me, but the spiritual reality was that I actually needed him to reject me as he did, so that I could find myself, erupt my inner strength, start the process of excavating who I really AM— what a gift he gave me. To this day, I thank God every day for the gift of his leaving.

I realized that I deserved better and to do better for me. I didn't need to sacrifice to be loved, real love is not suffering, true love is not supposed to hurt. I had been diminishing my light; shrinking my Spirit in order to be conditionally loved by the very individuals who kept reinforcing my feelings of unworthiness. I could never make them happy. No matter what I did, it was always not good enough. Talk about hitting a brick wall. It was a vicious negative pattern that I kept going in circles with until I was ready to get off the carousel. It was time!

Matchbox Twenty concert, July 19, 1997. A turning point for me. My friends and I were hanging out when a few guys came over to chat with us. A tall, thin, dark haired guy started talking to me; I felt confused as I usually was not the girl that guys talk to.

As I started to finally focus on my own thoughts and needs, that behavior no longer was a part of who I wanted to be and I now welcomed the needed attention. His name was Brady. Brady showered me with attention and compliments. He loved my glasses and asked if I was a lawyer. I know what you are thinking - I didn't care if it was a line - Brady was just what I needed. He was flirty and he appreciated my appearance. He told me how smart I looked and how beautiful I was. He told me I was super sexy! I had never been showered with as many compliments from a guy before!

Brady and I danced all night to the band. At the end of the concert, I said good night to him and left. He never asked for my number. He just said goodbye and nice to meet you. When I left the concert hall, I was walking on air. I knew Brady was heaven sent. What resonated the most for me was the feeling that he didn't want anything from me— he didn't take from me. He actually gave to me and I was willing to receive. We enjoyed an evening together and that was it. No expectations. Brady gave me hope. He was the reminder and validation I needed that all was going to be okay. At that time, the attention validated the fact that I could go on. I started working through the fear of what it all meant to not be in relationship with Aaron. I had to start to focus on the life I wanted, not on what I was told to do or believe.

I finally realized what drew me to Aaron. It had been a direct reflection of how I felt about myself. I thirsted for Aaron's love and acceptance. I felt high on the love when he was loving, but in those moments of his disregard (and there were many) I was on extreme lows. I mistook the comfort that I felt with him for love. Aaron's actions and words were often cruel and disrespectful; the mirror to my own self-talk. He was the reflection in my own lack of self-esteem and the belief that my worthiness was dependent on another's validation. In the end, he helped me to save myself. He was right; I was too good for him. I was too good to live a life of sadness and abuse. I was done fighting. I finally closed the door on the relationship with Aaron.

After 20 years of growth and self-exploration, the pain and disappointment from the past can still haunt me. I no longer feel the shudder of shame in my body, but the thoughts of my past self still does come up just a little bit. I have focused on healing and loving myself and letting go of the shame. It was time to forgive myself for allowing myself to experience such unhappiness and abuse. To move forward into the ability to love openly and freely, I had to forgive myself and surrender to the process of forgiveness. All the ugly truths had to be felt before I could actually let go. The fear of being lost in that pain was great. Through this process, I started to feel the faith and trust that I intrinsically knew to be truth in God. I realized that my fear was that, I wasn't good enough to be loved by God. How ridiculous is that! Talk about believing in a lie. I know Creator/Source/God loves me no matter what. God knows why

I make the choices I make, even when I don't have the conscious awareness of them. It is all part of the infinite plan of the life contract that I made on a soul level with God. So I ask myself, how can I be "bad" to God? How am I "not good enough" if God gives me permission through my own free will to experience life – the good, the bad, and the ugly? God knows the root cause of all our choices. He can look at us humans and give love and forgiveness, as He knows it is all for our soul's growth and learning.

It is painful for us when we turn away from the Light Source within our own being. The magical truth is that Aaron's rejection was my salvation. He saw my light. He knew I deserved much better than he could give me. He saw what I couldn't see within myself. Throughout the 10 years we spent together, he told me every time he broke it off with me– YOU deserve better! At the time, I was too afraid and too blind to own my magnificence– I needed to experience the growth and lessons– NOW I understand. I am filled with extreme gratitude. I start every day with gratitude. I thank Aaron, myself and God (and not in that specific order).

I had always been told that I was ordinary. That I was just a normal girl– nothing special. I learned that I had betrayed myself by forcing myself to fit into a box of normal and ordinary in hopes of feeling loved, while the love I so desperately needed was already deep within ME.

RIGHT! I am no ordinary girl. I am an extra-ordinary being!

I am a child of the universe, created in the likeness of the Creator. I am wondrous and special. A unique being infinitely connected to the rest of the universe and all its beings with a great purpose.

My purpose is to love. It is my life's journey to overcome the safety of playing small. I desire to own my greatness. I RISE to live my purpose with the highest vibration of love and service to the Divine.

Hallelujah.

Angela Catenaro McNeill is a freedom explorer and spiritual anthropologist who loves seeking and growing in spiritual truths while helping others to reveal their unique light. Angela is a mom, Energy Healer, Spiritual Life Coach, certified Yoga teacher, offering programs, retreats, and workshops for all ages.

Lucia Colangelo

The Venetian Mask

In the way of all love stories... there is never an end. Love will forever be felt not only in the hearts of the lovers, but of anyone whose lives were singed by the flames. Branded by heat for eternity.

But Love is tightly woven with its sibling Hate. The tragic star-crossed of ancient mind, the term that lived, throughout time. We like to think this fairy tale survived, that Hate is destroyed by his sister Love. Sadly, in truth, Hate is superior in strength, growing viciously in power, feeding on the evil of the mortal mind.

It is no wonder then that it was once believed, that star-crossed lovers had been maligned by faulty stars, thwarted from the beginning, their destiny set-by the cruel hand of the third child Misery.

And so our story will begin, a modern twist on an age old crime, an expose of malicious satire.

The Grappa

I watched as the candle flared, waiting for the scent of vanilla to drape me like a silken scarf. Glancing at the table where just the other night I had dined with my four friends, basking in the comfort of long-time friendship. Sophia, the spiritual one, using the gifts she had been blessed with to help others; Ella widowed at a young age, traveling the difficult journey of redefining her life after tragedy struck; Flora, thriving in her art, the creativity flowing from her after she released herself from an unhappy marriage; and Lilly, whose restless energy was calmed when she found the answers in her heart. We had lived through much, since our fateful meeting as children. Marriages, divorces, addiction, children, disappointments, failures, successes, joys, love, death. Sharing laughter, tears, anger and hugs. Our bond unbreakable through time. My Vintage Collection, I called them fondly, because it had always been a gift of mine to pair wines with my friends. It was easy, the description of the wine chosen matching perfectly with the personality of the friend. As much as I appreciated wine, I knew that it was more the words that captivated me, that excited my mind like the intoxicating liquid inside the bottles.

Today locked away in my reflections, I knew it was time to ignite the feelings in my soul, release the silence that had been so suffocating. I was being drawn to the last bottle in the wine cabinet. Purposely left unopened the night of my dinner party. We had shared four bottles that night, each one representing one of my friends and where she was at that moment in her life. I had not yet been ready to share my bottle with them. I still wasn't. This one was for appeasing my thirst, alone.

The memories that the bottle would arouse, lured me like a relentless seduction. My bare feet felt exposed on the worn out wood floors, the soles of my feet like pillows softening the pain. My body beaten from the years of painting. Arthritis setting into the bones that had repeatedly been abused. My mind refused to accept the pain, unwilling to slow down, I cried in silence.

I picked up the bottle, chosen with my heart, the one that reminded me the most of our relationship. Grappa, not really a wine, but a spirited drink created from the discarded seeds, stalks, stems and skins of the grape. Perhaps, in my mind it was a hopeful symbol of our castoff love, that the dregs of our sadness could eventually become, like the grappa, a new creation, a fiery warmth with a potent strength. Pouring the unclouded liquid in the traditional cognac glass, I hesitated before raising it to my waiting senses, still unsure if I was ready to immerse myself in the scent that would bring my mind back to the better times, when our love too had been unclouded, our path together clear. The bouquet was pleasant, which meant it was well made, for the impurities would come out in the vapors. Sighing, I wondered about the aroma of our bootlegged love. My lips singed by the liquid flames, I could almost feel the vibrations of his bass, beating inside me, tangling with the rhythm of my heart... and I remembered.

It was never about Love

I was infatuated. Mesmerized by eyes so blue I could see his soul. We mingled together like the stems of the most beautiful flowers... feeding them life. Unaware of the thorns that were hiding beneath.

We were inseparable. I was his rock... where he climbed to when his depression threatened to drown him. I became his medication, soothing the pain of his mind. Even in the darkest days the love stayed alive... although, it was never about love. Because love was the only thing we knew we would always have.

Maybe it was too deep, too desperate, too volatile, we should have known it would explode into chaos. But even if we had known about the fire... we wouldn't have cared. The danger of getting charred from the heat didn't scare us... we were untouchable.

We met through his passion for music and my desire to dance after a marriage of standing still. We touched a part of each other that our previous spouses had not even known existed. He played the bass, I was the quiet one at the side of the stage. The other girls dancing seductively in front of the band. Pulling tops up exposing breasts to entice. I just swayed to the sounds... confident in my ability to intrigue with my presence. My eyes leaving him only to smile at my admirers, letting them know with a look that I was taken.

He was seeking wild and I was radiating it. We took from each other. But it didn't take away from ourselves... the more we took the more we became.

The simple things were our air. Fishing trips filled with laughter. Freezing on the boat at 6:00 a.m. Eating buns stuffed with prosciutto, mortadella, salami, cheese. Eaten with hunger and greed, like our kisses in the morning fog. Our laughter echoing on the quiet lake as we drank beer from coffee mugs. Sunburnt noses by noon. The fish caught lost in my mind, all I remember is the sound of the water, the smell of the weeds growing tall above it, the scent of minnows, the heat of the sun.

Docking at the marina to sit under an umbrella. Buying lunch because we had eaten ours for breakfast. Cold beers in icy glasses while the local band played in the background. Then an afternoon of passion. Laying in each other's arms on the hard floor of the boat, our bodies not feeling the heat from the sun because the sun was cold compared to temperature of Us.

Cool nights in the cabin, cooking spaghetti and drinking wine. The signs everywhere warning of bears and the dangers of bringing food outdoors. Whispering nervously, we sat on the picnic bench, by a crackling bonfire, the darkness our invisible cloak, the stars our guests, two bodies touching, daring the bears to come. It was the best pasta we had ever eaten.

Our road trips to fishing destinations were filled with hours of chatter and silent conversation. Laughing hysterically at the icing sugar covering our clothes and faces from the jelly donuts we devoured with pleasure. The coffee hot and surprisingly calming. Were we each other's tranquilizer?

He became obsessed with whatever catch was on his mind that day. Trying lure after lure, the elusive trophy his goal. I fished by his side, more patient, calmed by the challenge not the catch.

Tired after a long day we made love in our bed, our bodies still rocking like the waves beneath the boat.

And then the storms blew in with such a vengeance, a force so fierce it altered the alignment of the stars, until they crossed and changed the direction of their destiny. Shaping not only the lives in its path, but shifting the form of the stars, from six points to eight, from energy and light to chaos and suffering.

The Storms

And then the storms blew in. I shivered as the visions of bliss turned quickly to images of destruction, almost slamming me down with their viciousness. Neglected mental illness is ruthless, cruelly destroying all that it touched. His eyes blazing judgment, shaming me timid. I became the blame, for all he thought wrong in his life, belittling who I was, to justify his actions. He tied his medication that was me around a rock and threw it into the abyss. Refusing help, denying he needed it. I took the blame in defense of his illness and lost myself. I floated outside my being, emotions raw, confused, I had given him my love in innocence and it had been misused. But mental illness grows where it is seeded, and will always seek out those who fed it. So he ran to his past, where he thought he was free, but the chains of his addiction grew tighter with restriction.

We lived in a haze of alcohol and drugs, each searching for salvation, each finding none. Until the night we exploded with words, all the pent up emotions gushing through the wounds of our souls. In the aftermath of tears and accusations, with the calming hand of the law in control, we realized we needed to decide where we would go. So we parted homes, our lives in shambles, torn apart by the shards of our turmoil.

Romantic tragedy? Or tragic romance? Could the belief that the position of the stars ruled our fate be true? Or is our destiny governed by our behavior?

Perhaps this was not a tale of stars crossed in a path. In truth, it seemed to be, the stars that were Lucia and her Giuliano, had in fact collided. Brought together by the forces of gravity.

But their love defied natures law, and as the fragments of their stellar explosion reunited on earthly ground, the warmth from the fiery ball of flames filled their souls, their hearts, their love.

The Illusion

As I poured myself another grappa and sat down, exhausted from the exertion of my thoughts, I knew the memories would fade with time but they determined who we were forever. Tears stained my face with grief at all that I had endured through those turbulent times. My visions took me to the scene that had defined us. When the shards of our love had lay glowing at our feet, tempting us with their brilliance. The weight of sadness lightened, as we stood united, watching the alcohol swirling down the drain, the pills disposed of, and the fog beginning to rise. Life without each other had been no decision at all, our hearts had won that battle, because, it was never about love.

And then my two, his three, became our five. Children from a different love, blended together like the vines of the grape, tangled in all their glory and woe. Our home filled with laughter and tears, angry moments of rivalry, teasing and fears. Late night movies, messy rooms, too much food, not enough time. We bonded in simplicity, because, souls don't judge when strangers meet.

We changed our ways, Giuliano and I, dwelling in goodness, harmony and love. Treating each other with the word that binds, Respect it seems had arrived just in time. We lazed in bed, spent hours sharing words, recapturing each other with adventures, passion and food.

We planned our future, our dreams within reach, made plans for tomorrows, forgetting the yesterdays. It was a time of revitalization, fusing in our minds the knowledge that we were soul mates from the start. That nothing could take away the gift that was 'Us.'

Yet the storm it seemed would not subside, the origin changed but the same target still its eye. There were some that continued to blame, condemned me for the courage to stand up for my name. They hated the fact that I cloaked him with strength and forbade my existence, my presence, my breath.

Enter the Mask, the master of deception, used in ancient Venetian times to conceal the identity of those frolicking, promiscuous lust, escaping judgment by anonymity. Walking freely as equals, intimidating, mysterious, frightening or humorous, the wearer decides the cause of the day. Each unique and beautiful in its own way. Never intended to hurt or betray, it eventually became restricted in the average day, then used only during periods of carnival folly.

Yet a more dangerous mask has been unleashed amongst us, an invisible one sheathed in the hearts of cowards. Used to deceive and betray with disguise. Its power untamed is surpassed by no evil, its weapon, the Tongue.

The Venetian Mask

Reaching gently in the cabinet drawer, I pulled out the three fragile objects, wrapped in soft pink, mint green and sky blue tissue paper. As I revealed the unnerving features of the first mask hidden under the blue wrapping, The Bauta, I shivered at the coldness seeping from the hollow gaps that were meant to be for the wearers eyes. We had bought it in a moment of silliness, a way to soften the darkness his family cast. We had not known that in the end it would be the symbol of the carnage of our love.

The Venetian mask, the illusion of anonymity, the wearer concealing emotions with frozen features, but the eyes always revealed, the speakers of the soul. This one to me was the most dangerous. Covering the whole face, with a large stubborn chin and jaw, it was used traditionally with a cape, ensuring that the wearer was fully disguised. By law no weapons were to be worn while wearing this mask, but the law had forgotten the damage of words, spoken through echoing sounds, intensified by eyes as empty as the cavities they stared from.

I had picked this one for them. Understanding deeper than Giuliano the significance of the impact it would have on us. The Bauta, for the cowards hiding behind the mask, afraid to feel the truth, judging all through their barren eyes. Those so dead in their lives that they only feel alive with the taste of blood on their poisonous tongues. They couldn't forgive me for standing up to their son, their brother, the night our world erupted in bleeding words. They choose to close their eyes at the transformation we created, at the confidence and strength he was gaining with our love now purified. So they maimed, scarring my heart with barbed tongues. Words uttered with no shame, no conscience, their intent was to hurt me.

I had been outcast and discarded. Six years of my loving them forgotten in their hate, their betrayal of me. I loved the man they had created from a boy, his children tucked deep in my soul. They could not see that they had failed him, allowing him to wallow in his weakness, or perhaps they did see, but preferred to be blind. They hated that I saw the truth, the control they seek over him and his children, a sickness created out of misery not love. They were happier destroying.

As Giuliano and I overcame our failings and our love grew brighter, their hate grew uglier. Jealous of the family we created with our children, they grew more desperate, more dangerous. They wanted him and his children under their roof, their watch, their rules. Had they created the disease that now festered in Giuliano's mind? Resentful of my strength and our growing bond, they relentlessly attacked, until too weary to defend, our family torn, shredded to dust. Destroying lives they said mattered to them, all for one, that they said didn't.

Their empty souls couldn't see the weeping hearts of our innocent children, who had flourished and thrived with the love in our happy home. The children who could feel the betrayal too and saw the destruction it caused. They were helpless to speak in my defense, waiting for a sign from Giuliano to guide them, he failed them too. His family had tarnished the shine on an otherwise brilliant love and they danced amongst the flames.

Words spoken by fools are the cruelest at best
causing havoc around them
not giving a rest
until they destroy into dust
what was once a pure light
till darkness becomes
they set off sparks that ignite
like flames in a fight
hurting and growing stronger with each soul it engulfs
sticks and stones will bruise and cut
then mend like they never were

names will haunt forever etched in pain that never subsides
no relief from the agony of the sharpened tongue
steel cuts through bone
blades whirling till to deep
the sound ruthless in its power
leaving scars like tattoos for life
there is no cure for the evil voice
it screams its cry
mingling with the blood of those
whose pieces are left to die
in pools of sadness
and spirits cry

Giuliano's Mask

It was the thorns that had pierced us dry in the end, bleeding our love into puddles of dried ugly nothingness. The same flowers that had mesmerized and captured had unleashed their talons upon us. His family.

They pulled the strings of his heart until they unraveled into a tanged mess of confusion. His emotions twisted, he faded away, finding comfort in the mask they pushed his way. He wore it well Giuliano, deceiving even my soul, which was once one with his. The mask we bought to protect him from his mental ails, the Plague Doctor Mask (the memento mori) white, with a long hollow beak, round black holes where the eyes would see, bespectacled with crystals. Once used to ward off illness and death, it has now become the very symbol of it. Staring at me from its coffin of green tissue, I felt my heart seize.

He built a home with me, one he never kept his promise of forever in. He abandoned me, our children, our future, leaving me on my knees in the rubble of our crumbling home. Giuliano was not the assailant I agree, but an accomplice in his silence, could he not see? That a word from him would have dulled the blades? Yet his silence sharpened the edges, the roar of the blades whirling, can he sleep at night? Knowing that his quietness mingled with the screams from my pain, his blood soaked hands holding what was once my heart. The pain will live on, because no salve can comfort once the heart has been ripped apart.

He took the mask we bought with love, on our last trip to Venice, and hid his truth behind it. Making a mockery of us. He walked out. Left without a word! Like I was nothing! Worthless! I was once again the blame, because he couldn't stand the pressure of choosing between living life with me and the demands his family made on him. So he ran to them on the night that was to be our beginning! Our home sold, we were writing our future with different colored markers, improving our finances, planning our retirement in Florida. Looking at brochures for family trips, cottages, wedding destinations.

Years of together gone in a second. Jarred and in shock, I woke up to blankness, a world without light. The me of before thrown away through the night. In a heartbeat I vanished, from all I had known, from the souls in my blood, to the hollows of my bones. My heart still alive, I crawled out of my skin, floated up to the sky, and watched myself cry.

I would have fought the world for our love, but I'm not fighting him to love me.

My Mask

The Bauta and The Plague Doctor stared up at me from their fragile beds, the hot poisonous fumes weeping from them almost visible to my clouded eyes. I had always had a fascination with Venetian Masks. The symbol of my favorite city. Since my first visit to Venice as a child, when I had stared at the masked revelers I had fallen in love with the mystery, the passion, the romance, seeing only the beauty, unaware in my innocence of the deceiving duality its wearer was capable of.

Shivering as I rewrapped the two masks, I tucked them away into a corner of the cabinet.

I held my breath as I bared the exquisite Columbina Mask. My mask. Pink with delicate wispy feathers, encrusted with shimmering crystals, its slanted cat eyes eerily vacant. I walked to the mirror, fastening the half mask around my head with the silky ribbons. I had picked this one because pink was my favorite color, and it had also been my mama's. Looking over at the lovely black and white sketch of her that hung in a special place on the wall, I hoped that heaven had shielded my mama from having to watch me in pain.

I smiled sadly at my image, remembering the sensual love making we had shared that night in Venice. When I had walked to our bed wearing the mask and the Juliet inspired gown that barely concealed my passion, his eyes had blazed love. We had awoken with limbs entwined like the clothes of a mummy, protected for eternity. A shield against the elements our foolish hearts believed.

I removed the mask, not wanting to be saddened by things that could never be again. I still adore venetian masks, even though I had been the victim of their abuse. The masks really only a symbol of the betrayal, I would forever be weary of the wearer.

I had risen above the ashes of evil and turned my world into a place where love, hope, happiness, tears, laughter, fears and sorrow were felt without judgment.

As the scents of life filled my emptiness with warmth, the storms calmed and beams of hope bounced around like fairies alive. I not only breathed to live, but lived to breathe and be. When the chaos of my mind shifted, my emotions tangled together, not in fear and uncertainty, but in shyness and wonder. Was this the me I had lost when I started to believe that I deserved all the things they said and did to me? Clearly seeing the path, still I hesitated, could it be this easy? Until I realized that living was about peeking through the blinds of life, daring to allow the light in, staring at the darkness the shade provides and bravely whispering, "I'm ready."

The hurt, pain, and embarrassment subsided, as the truth was revealed to our world. His excuses about money laughed back in his face. It was now understood that I could be worth millions, but in the minds of his family, I would always be worthless. And by him leaving me for them, he had stamped my heart the same.

I realized that he couldn't or wouldn't give me the two things that would make our forever complete, respect and commitment.

But my heart was meant to beat, to live and to love.

I started slowly to forgive the Giuliano that had decided to hide what was true. Because it was never about love and it was never about me. The hate his family had, was really in themselves. He had been raised and manipulated with abusive control. Standing up for myself had frayed the ropes they tried to bind me with, and fearful that my strength would seep into him, they choose to cut me loose with sharpened tongues. But could soul mates created by the stars really be destroyed by human minds?

Because still Giuliano came back to me, unable to stay away, eyes filled with tears, defeated, shoulders heaving with the weight of guilt. Unable to live without me, he lured with sips from his poison love. And I drank, my soul thirsty for him. The stars still not giving up on us, our love fluttering a beat, a tiny pulse refusing to be destroyed, so what could I do? When all I had left was that tiny beat of him? Did I silence it too?

Once again we were one, the same in a different way. Stars once again aligned, our love so explosive it left us shaking but alive. Weekends away, movies, wine, dinners filled with hopes and dreams, goodnight kisses from afar.

And that's where our paths collided, in kisses from afar. Giuliano still not brave enough to defend his one true love. For he could not understand that you could love someone with your heart and soul but if your mind is controlled by someone else your destined to be alone.

I was stronger now, and demanded to know, why I, a creation of soul mates myself, was not good enough in his eyes to walk by his side with pride. So I whispered in heartache that I would be dishonoring my parents love, if I agreed to stay silent about our renewed love. Giuliano's family had discovered it, our forebidden reunion and attacked him like vultures swarming from the skies. I refused to be hidden, a shameful secret. My new found confidence refusing to be constrained by the same evil minds that had crushed me before. I understood that our love was a gift, but until he released himself from their grip it would never be true.

He either stood by my side, our love visible to all, or I walked the path alone, twinkling amongst the other stars.

Once again he was gone, unable to rise, but this time I didn't cry. Because the words that you see here took the place of those tears, and became immortalized in ink created from the dust of falling stars.

Our story would no longer remain a mystery locked in our hearts, the world would know of our great love and how the winds of evil had taken hold of Giuliano, until he was no more.

There are those that choose to live life clawing their way through an intricate, suffocating and binding web of lies, secrets, hate and judgment. Their bodies suffering with illnesses and ailments from the poisonous fumes their madness produces. Blind to truth, honesty, love, joy and happiness, they spend their days luring victims into their torturous chambers. Their evil, a darkness so black it confuses the senses. Because strategy by fools puts innocence in front and lives are lost to hate. But only the weak will succumb. The survivors will rejoice in freedom and light. United together in strength... in love.

Unmasked

Giuliano sat frozen, locked away in his mind, terrified that words would ignite the feelings in his soul. His silence comforting. His body cold. He no longer loved, his heart beating but not alive.

His world without me not worth living. A puppet that did as the strings commanded. Passion no longer familiar, his body grew old, shriveled up in the heat of aloneness. And still the shadows of those who conquered lurked behind him, always watching.

I lifted the bottle of grappa, its power heady as I felt the sway of intoxication, I wanted its effects tonight. To extinguish the memories and celebrate new beginnings. The blessings I had been given when I opened myself to them had filled my universe with opportunity and magic. I was writing daily now, my work starting to gain recognition as it was published. Cherished friendships renewed through good food and wine. The men I dated would stay friends for now, my purpose was creating me, one day at a time.

My vintage friends stayed true, swaddling me in a cocoon, releasing only when my wings could fly, but always ready to catch me if I faltered in the sky.

Tangled lies, false truths, all left behind. Soul mates may be linked without choice, but once one betrays, the other gains the strength of both.

As I was pouring, I felt but couldn't stop, the loosening of my grip on the bottle. I watched fascinated as it splashed precious liquid on my bare feet, the glass pieces shattering like my heart once had.

The mess cleaned up, I knew it was time. It had been awhile since I had paired myself with wine. I needed a lively, fresh new creation, an acknowledgement of the Me I was Born to Be. I choose the colorful black, red and plum bottle, Bodacious, 2014, Canadian. Remarkable, sensual, audacious, gutsy, it was the spirit flowing from me.

Pouring a glass of the ruby liquid I made my way to the garden and sat on one of the comfortable chairs that surrounded the fire pit. One of my favorite places, I now lit the always ready logs and watched as they kindled and sparked alive. Tilting my head back to sip, I lingered on the sky above. As I gazed at the stars, they didn't cross, they didn't collide. Then I squinted in disbelief, my heartbeat suspended, because for a second, a blink, the stars had glowed in the vision of two masks, and in the blackest of skies, the images seemed to be connected by two hearts, bravely beating in the night, and as I watched in awe, those two hearts collided and then disappeared into nothing.

Lucia Colangelo is the International Bestselling author of the inspirational 'My Vintage Collection' found in The Sisterhood ƒolios Live Out Loud. 'The Venetian Mask' is the dark, intense second instalment in the trilogy. She is currently working on the third enchanting story titled 'Non Ti Scordar Di Me (Forget Me Not), which will be featured in The Sisterhood ƒolios Ignite Your Inner Warrior.

She writes with passion and creativity; her love for words expressed in the images she creates in the minds of her readers. Her unique style continues to capture the imagination. Lucia lives in Toronto with her family. When she's not writing she enjoys traveling, reading, gourmet pizza, pasta, lattes and wine.

Laura DeGasperis

You are worthy of your dreams

I always wondered how those people, who looked liked they had all their shit together, did it? I envied those who had the perfect job, beautiful dream home and they looked effortlessly put-together. I had a small house with simple furniture. I wore bargain clothes and hand-me-downs from friends and family. It is not that I was broke, I was living within my means. I felt guilty spending even a dollar on myself, knowing that it could've gone to putting food in my family's mouth or paying a bill. When my birthday or Christmas came around, I would get excited because I knew that if I received money or gift cards, that it would just toward paying the bills or buying something for my husband. I never used them on myself, even though I wanted to. This was the way it was, day in and day out, year after year. I was grateful to have a roof over my head, but I always dreamed of something more. I didn't want to simply wish for it, but I wanted to earn those things simply by hard work and determination. I tried to put my intention into the universe but it didn't come. What was I missing? Was there some magic spell or words? What was I doing wrong? I knew that those things didn't come easy, and I was going to have to work hard to achieve it. I would think back to those people, I thought had it all. Was it that they were just lucky and that luck had just simply forgotten all about me? Maybe Karma was taking its time to finally get to me. I asked myself these questions everyday and they were never answered.

I went to college twice and both times found entry-level positions with minimal pay. I found myself perpetually in the last-in-first-out policies of employment which prompted me to feel like I wasn't the model employee. This took a huge toll on my ego and my self-confidence. Each time I had aspirations and dreams of making it far up the corporate ladder but no matter how hard I tried, I would always end up starting all over again. It was frustrating trying to be the new person and having to prove myself once again. I also had to build new work relationships with people who were strangers. I would just continue on every day. I put my big girl pants on and kept doing what I could do to make my mark and it became exhausting. My soul became tired, my confidence crushed by self-blame. I began to believe that it was my entire fault and no one thought I was good enough. My drive once again extinguished by being laid off once again.

The last time was different. My husband and I finally settled into our second home. We sacrificed being close to the city by moving an hour away so that we could have a larger home to start our family. I didn't mind being closer to farms and nature. My drive home from work put me at peace as I drove by the rolling fields of green and amber. My husband had a great union job as an electrician and I found a place I could make a mark for myself in the building industry. I was also 5 weeks pregnant. I knew that I would give it the typical three months before I let them know, but before I knew it, I was called into the boss's office with the same excuse. I heard it many times before but this time it was hard to take and I broke down in her office. I told her I was pregnant but I realized that wouldn't have made any difference and I accepted my fate. On my drive home, all my hopes and dreams came crushing down once again. This time, I had a baby on the way and didn't know what to do. I felt like I disappointed my husband, family and my new baby on the way.

What kind of mom was I going to be if I couldn't even keep a job for more than six months? I felt like a complete failure. I sobbed all the way home.

I tried to look for a job— something, anything, but nothing came my way. I remember one day feeling the pangs of deceit and guilt knowing that I would be leaving as soon as someone took me on. As time went on I decided to give up. The stress wasn't doing me or the baby any good, so I decided to take it easy and wait for my baby to come. Little did I know my baby had other plans.

It was a hot and humid July Sunday morning. I was finishing up some invitations for my baby shower and my husband was working so I decided to have a nap. When I awoke, I had the worst cramping and hoped a shower would ease the pain. I was 28 weeks pregnant and didn't even think of the possibility of an early delivery. I noticed that I was spotting when I was in the shower and decided not to chance it and called the triage at the local hospital. They advised me to come in to get checked just in case. We waited a bit for the doctor to see us and when he checked my cervix he was shocked that I was three centimeters dilated. The most fear inducing moment of my life was when the doctor walked away with a complete sense of shock and blood all over his hands. He proceeded to tell us that they don't deliver babies there earlier than thirty weeks because they didn't have the resources or the NICU to handle such a delivery. I was going to be taken by helicopter to the nearest high risk hospital.

I wasn't ready for this, mentally or physically. I went into shock and wanted to check out mentally. I didn't want to deliver her, not now. I wasn't ready but I had no choice. Once I landed, my parents and sister were there waiting for me, but not my husband Mike. He was still stuck in traffic and I prayed that he would be there in time. I remember them asking me who I wanted in the delivery room if my husband didn't make it in time. I asked for my mother because she did this twice before and should be used to this sort of stuff. Well little did I know the relief she had when Mike made it in time!

July 15, 2013 at 1:05 a.m., my daughter was born, twelve weeks early, weighing only 2lbs, 5oz. She was so tiny but she cried the second she entered this world. It was her warrior cry, her message for me to not worry and that she's "got this." The first time I got to see her was a couple hours later. She was so wrinkled and her skin was red. She was attached to so many little wires and tubes that were there to keep her alive. I remember staring at her in the incubator one day looking at all the technology it took to replicate what the human body can do in our wombs. It was incredible and made me feel blessed that I was able to create her from my body.

The next night after everything settled and I was in the quiet and still of my hospital room, I sat there in my bed crying. I held my empty womb riddled with guilt that my daughter was fighting to stay alive because my body wasn't strong enough to hold her. I quietly sobbed while my husband slept in the bed next to me. I felt that this was my fault and didn't want to burden him with my guilt. He had enough to worry about being the sole provider at the time, and was going to be headed to work the very next day because if he didn't work, he didn't get paid. The next sixty-one days in the hospital were going to be the hardest days of his life.

Every morning we would wake up early and I would drop him off at work and head to the hospital to spend time with Emily.

I would then pick him up and we would head back to the hospital to spend the rest of the evening with her until we were too tired, and headed back home to sleep and prepare for the next day.

The most difficult day was when we were told that Emily had a brain bleed from the delivery and that they couldn't give us any answers to her future development. The doctors told us that we would just have to wait and see. Thoughts raced through my head. Is my daughter brain damaged? Will she forever be developmentally delayed? I had no clue. I decided not to enlist in the help of 'Dr. Google' and instead picked the brains of the nurses and doctors, even though they didn't like to give any advice because they simply had no idea what her outcome could be. So we just waited.

Emily came home September 12, 2013. One month earlier than my due date and right on Mike's birthday. They told us don't expect her to be home before her due date but Emily surpassed all expectations and gave her daddy the best birthday gift. She was still less than 5lbs when we brought her home but breathing and eating all on her own. I felt that the battle was over and I won. My daughter was home, she was healthy and we could now move on to the next chapter of our lives. One big happy family. Little did I know the storm that was waiting over head.

I knew during my stay in the hospital, that I was dealing with some post-partum anxiety and decided to seek out professional help. The official diagnosis was PTSD, post-partum anxiety and depression. I thought that once I got home it would get better. I was wrong, and it only got worse. Combining the diagnosis with, sleep deprivation, lack of appetite and isolation and I was nearly ready to give up. I loved my daughter but I hated the toll it was taking on me mentally, emotionally and physically. I loved being Emily's mom but I just hated being what I thought society wanted me to be as a mom. I hated my husband because he was able to escape to work or sleep through the night. I hated a lot of things.

It took me a while to be around full-term pregnant women. The psychiatrist told me that it was similar to mourning a loss. I lost out on being full-term pregnant. Having that moment when your baby is born and placed on your chest and you bond in that special moment. I had one melt down in an IKEA when I saw a full-term pregnant lady complain to the cashier in front of me that she couldn't wait until her baby came out as she was tired of carrying him. And they laughed. I fought back tears and my husband gripped my hand. My daughter was fighting for her life because my body was weak and couldn't carry her. It was not those ladies fault. They didn't know what I had just gone through. It did get a lot easier as time went on. I got to experience all the other aspects of pregnancy and being a mother. I got to have her naturally, something they didn't think I could do full-term being high risk. And for what it's worth, I can still remember her first kicks and all the cravings I had when I was pregnant with her.

I learned to be very humble with my losses and gains. I had the best of a bad situation. Yes, Emily was three months early but we never had any setbacks. She just ate, slept and grew. I remember leaving the NICU one night after learning about Emily's brain bleed and seeing another mother crying in the arms of her husband. All her family surrounded her and I saw her in her most vulnerable moment. She had given birth to twins and her baby boy had passed. My heart broke for her, really broke. Not in the "oh man I feel bad for her" and continued on with my life way. I cried all the way home, sobbing in my hands for my pain and her loss. Why did this happen to us, to all of us moms here in this NICU? People who never had any experience like these, always tell me, that they couldn't have ever handled that happening to them. They ask how I was able to do it. The truth is, I couldn't, but did it anyways. You just wake up and do it, again and again until it becomes your new 'normal.'

My new 'normal,' as I mentioned, was not all that easy to transition into. I was happy that I had amazing friends and family members that helped out when they saw how overwhelmed I was.

One person who was pivotal in helping me transition was my good friend Helen. She is, and continues to be a mentor in my life. During one of our chat sessions, two epiphanies happened. First, she told me that I had nothing to do with Emily coming early, that was just her journey and that she was the one who determined it so. I had to stop blaming myself for that and move on, once I could accept that, it would be easier to move on and live a life of joy and follow my passion. Second, that I was meant to write. When she told me that, I just laughed it off. I wasn't a writer. I did not go to university or college to graduate with any diplomas in literature or writing. She suggested to start writing a journal to Emily and go from there. I did confide in her something that I had been writing a journal ever since I was a child. I would create worlds and stories in my head. I would even take books or movies and create different story lines or endings. This happened all my life, everyday, anytime I had a moment to be lost in my thoughts. I thought there was something wrong with me. I was always lost in thoughts, and that I should get my head out of the clouds. Little did I know, it was my calling to write. I think Helen wanted to shake some sense into me at that moment. "Girl that is your higher self telling you to write", she said.

There was one thing that should have been an indication of what my passion was, but I never really thought that I was really good at. Thoughts came rushing back to me as early as second grade, when I would staple together lined paper and create stories. When kids in fourth grade were writing stories about their dogs and ice cream adventures, I wrote a mystery of who killed the gym teacher. Morbid, I know. I had such an interesting imagination but didn't realize that this was something that I was meant to spend the rest of my life doing.

At some point in a person's life, they can recollect time when they experience that moment of a weight lifted from their shoulders. Something I always thought was a metaphor. But at that moment, I felt a literal shift in the pressure in my body. It was as if an anchor that was holding me down has somehow released, and I was able to float and move on my own once more.

I left that session with an eagerness to pursue my new found passion. Like a toddler fearlessly eager to walk on their own not realizing there will eventually come a moment when they will fall. As I began to write, numerous fears began to surround me. "What if you're not good enough?" "You don't know how to even structure a novel or even good at grammar for that matter." "What if your stories stink?" "Just forget about it."

I let all the fears come and go and when I had that moment of quiet, a tiny voice still remained. It asked me to tell it a story, and I did. I began to write and let it flow like water out of my mind and into the computer. I remembered back to what my teacher said when I was applying for Interior Design school about how the technical aspects of things can be taught but the creativity comes from within. It's funny how some things that we learn along the way follow us and direct us in times of hesitation.

I decided not to get myself focused on the perfect editing for my writings, but to just get the ideas down.

It took me a while to write even just a chapter as I allowed life and responsibilities take precedence over my writing. Sometimes, not even writing for months on end. That is when I noticed, that the times I was not writing, I felt like something was missing. I had spent almost a year-and-a-half barely doing the one thing that brought me joy. Don't get me wrong, I loved the time I spent with my family and friends but the little thing that made me feel like myself, was taking the backseat to life again.

I decided to sit down and find a school that taught writing. This way I had to dedicate at least one day a week, minimum, to doing what I love to do. I found a writing course about an hour away but I signed up on a whim, something that I do not regret at all. I could never imagine that I would gain all the knowledge and support to actually start writing a novel. I felt that with learning all the technical elements to writing I would have the confidence to submit something into the world. Learning the technical aspects to writing was only one step towards following my dreams. There was more I needed to learn, and I was far from becoming the author I wanted to be.

One area of my life that I still had to overcome was my belief in myself. I never truly believed that I could contribute anything worthwhile. I had a notion that for one to make an impact in the world you had to affect millions of people. I knew that it can only take one person's life to change to make an impact and that person was me. I needed to understand that I was good enough to write something worth publishing. I needed to crush all my fears, one by one, until there was nothing to fear anymore. I began to think back to my hardest time in my life. I survived my struggles with PTSD and depression, and watching my daughter fight for her life in an incubator, but why is it that I couldn't put pen to paper and write a story to share? I once was told that we will all experience hardships in our lives, some easier than others, and when faced with the choice of living my life without writing or submitting something and inspiring just one person, well I knew what choice to make.

In time, I continued to surround myself with new people who would guide me to be a better person, stronger woman and someone worth believing in. These people taught me to believe that I have worth and a voice that could be heard. I learned that you could ask the universe for the very thing you wanted and would receive it. Sometimes, not always necessarily in the form you want, but that's what it does. I followed powerful successful women and read about historical women who made changes in this world. I learned that putting me first was not selfish, and that it made me a better mother, wife and friend. By building myself up first, I am stronger to raise my daughter to be an amazing woman in this world. I want her to follow her dreams, never doubt herself and believe that there is no limit to her potential. When I was giving a piece of myself to everyone, there was nothing left of me, and anything I did was never good enough. Believe that being selfish, is the most selfless thing you can do.

I believe that there does come a time in everyone's life that they realize their self-worth and understand that they are capable of following their dreams. I think for me not believing I am worthy to follow my dreams, is one of the major components that blocked me from ever realizing that I could be the writer that I should have been early on. There is no time limit to following your passions, there are people in their seventies, eighties and even nineties starting over and finally doing what they are meant to do. I am in my mid-thirties and feel that I'm so lucky to realize this early. I know now, that it's okay to start over as long as it's for a passion that makes you wake up every morning happy. If your passion inspires people and contributes to society in a positive way with integrity, then why shouldn't you do it? So often, our conversations consist of complaining we are tired, hate work and Mondays and live for our vacation time. We live by the "someday-one-day" mentality that never comes. Time is so precious and short and my hope for everyone that when their time is up, they have spent every day doing what they loved to do and shared it with the world. Yeah, I know preachy, but necessary.

I don't think anymore about the people that I thought had their shit all together. I don't focus on the material gains in life anymore. I focus on my goals of making myself and my family happy. I take pride that my hard work is going to something more monumental and can be passed on for generations. Following a passion gave me more meaning in my life than believing I needed to live this perfect life full of objects and things that would just expire. My dream house didn't become a beautifully designed mansion; it became a home with memories. The fancy clothes and nice hair became embracing a healthy and strong body. I began to desire other dreams and the harder I worked, the more obtainable they became. Did Karma finally remember me? I believe it showed me, that to truly be happy I needed to work hard towards the things that I needed, and not wanted.

I had an interesting story of something that happened to me. I had gone out for a walk around my neighborhood and I am a firm believer of asking the universe for what you want. Something came to mind and I asked the universe to go on an adventure. I wanted to do something fun in my life and it didn't have to be soon but I wanted something to remember for the rest of my life as the best adventure I ever been on. I only asked that in that moment to give me a sign that it would happen. In that moment a rabbit had crossed my path and hopped to the other side of the road. Both the rabbit and I stopped in our tracks. I stared at him in that moment and realized that the universe had heard me. I laughed out loud and the irony that the universe would speak to me in the manner that only I would realize. I recognized it instantly as the White Rabbit in one of my favorite childhood books, Alice in Wonderland. I looked up at the sky and smiled. I knew I would have to brace myself for the best adventure yet to come.

EMILY UPDATE

At the time of this publishing, Emily will be four years old. She is high average for her speaking and a very creative and happy child, something we are forever grateful for. We had some bumps along the way but the doctors, nurses and follow-up clinic at her hospital are incredible at acknowledging any delays and helping with them.

Laura DeGasperis is a mom to an amazing little girl, wife to her supportive husband and following her passion in writing. Laura enjoys time away with her family at the cottage where she can disconnect and unwind with a mojito. She loves yoga, spin classes, going to the theatre and expanding her knowledge with a variety of book genres.

Lauren Dickson

Monday's Child

A Mother Goose poem once stated that, "Monday's Child is fair of face." Well, in my case, it could also be added that this particular "Monday's Child" is an old, witty soul, and that of an empathetic and benevolent nature. Ever since I was a very small child, I have many times felt as though I was born at the wrong time, and didn't quite fit in. It took some time for me to realize that it wasn't all about fitting in, but rather standing out!

I believe it was a mix of my genetic and emotional makeup, as well as the experiences I have had, that resulted in developing anxiety and a form of depression. It had built up over time, and then piqued in my teenage years. I had this bubbly, witty, outgoing personality as a little girl that seemed to have dimmed by the age of seven. As if there was a shift, I became more shy and timid... in public anyway. There were changing factors in my life at the time, which contributed to this change in my self-expression; I was getting bullied at school, and my home life was in a bit of an uproar due to my parents often fighting. All of our extended family lived out of province, or out of country, so my four siblings and I didn't have a quiet haven to go to when the roaring yells would commence. As much as that strain between my parents affected myself and my siblings, there were also times where we would hide in our rooms, keeping ourselves occupied as if it was part of the norm. In sensing the tension in the house some days, I remember feeling the anxiety build up inside me. Then there were the nights I would lay in my bed, with the nervous feeling in the pit of my stomach of knowing that if I fell asleep, it would soon be interrupted by a chaotic disruption. I'm not saying there were never good times growing up; in fact, I have many good memories from my childhood. However, there was a lot of stress and chaos. There were nights we spent at a family friend's house because of the disturbances at home. Then one particular instance which lead to my parents having strict orders to have zero contact with each other for one year. That lack of communication between them meant that my siblings and I were the go-between for passing along messages back and forth. Needless to say, that caused stress and anxiety to build more within me.

As if that all wasn't stressful enough, my eldest brother tormented me. My dad was hard on him, and my brother seemed to have taken that out on me. Then, I was teased at school, for having been the "quiet, bookworm with glasses." It seemed as though everywhere I went, there was some sort of torment. That's not to say my entire childhood was miserable. (Trust me, if I could, I would rewind to the 90s and stay there... or the old soul in me would prefer to rewind a few decades prior to that, where it probably would have felt more fitting).

"It is both a blessing and a curse to feel
everything so very deeply."
~David Jones

Being born an old soul, I have also been a very sensitive, cautious, and empathetic person. I also remember being told as a child that I was very mature beyond my years. I think I carried more care and responsibility than what was good for me. It would break my heart to see someone else hurting, or even disappointed for not getting something they wanted. I've always wanted to make sure others were taken care of and happy. As sweet and loving as that gesture and good-hearted nature is, it also takes a toll on you emotionally; as it is impossible to always please everybody else. There were times where if I was conflicted on making a decision, I would go with what my mother or someone else would kindly suggest, even if it wasn't exactly what I had wanted— thinking that I would disappoint them if I did otherwise, only to later find out that was not the case.

By the age of fifteen, depression and anxiety had started to really hit me. It affected my concentration and motivation in school, when I was otherwise a stellar student. I lacked the energy to want to get up in the morning, and test papers often took me longer to complete as I found myself having to read over questions a few times for me to fully think straight. Days felt long and tiring as I would wait for that bell to release me from another day of which just felt empty. By the time I got home, most days I would cry quietly in my room, sometimes without even knowing why. There were nights where I would lay awake from my mind being on a constant spin cycle of worries, and thoughts. Then, there were other times where I could sleep and sleep, and it felt like it was never enough. I often felt misunderstood and unheard, and to make myself feel better, that I would quietly talk aloud to myself with no one else around; as if someone was there to hear me... just to feel like I could state my piece. Some would wonder why I would talk so passionately and loudly about certain topics, as I wanted to get out what I had to say while I could! I wanted my thoughts and opinions said out loud without being interrupted, or belittled for being "little Lauren." I wasn't as quick to defend myself back then. I would often run off and cry or my feelings would come out in an angry form, for the frustration I was feeling. I had what seemed to be the longest tension headache ever, as it had lasted the better part of a year. I was so scared that I was sick! I was scared that this rut I was in was a never-ending tunnel of darkness; only to much later realize that it was this "darkness" that lead me to a much brighter, illuminating light!

At the age of 18, I sought counseling to help me cope with my struggles. I was hesitant at first, not wanting to tell my life story to a complete stranger. I would think to myself that, they didn't know me, so how could they possibly begin to comprehend the glass cage of emotion which I found myself trapped in, with what seemed at the time to be no way out?

One thing I am grateful for about my struggles, is that, it was never so severe to the point where I considered suicide, or hurting myself in any way. I was hurting, yes. I was afraid, lonely, stuck, and confused. Were there times I felt so uncomfortable in my own body and wanted to jump out of my own skin? You bet; but to hurt myself? Never! Despite the pain, and the physically, emotionally and mentally draining sensation, I still knew I was meant for so much more.

I often tried to hide my tears, and would quietly sob in my room so no one else could hear. When my mom saw me crying, her reaction sometimes came across as angry, or frustrated, which made me feel even more lonely and misunderstood. She didn't know why I was upset, so that confusion caused her response to sometimes come across as insensitive. In more recent years, my mother had told me that she wished she had known and understood more of what I was going through, so as to help me, and to help my then teachers better understand my struggles. I often found that with most of my family anyways. The "oh there's Lauren crying again." Or, "what's wrong with Lauren." Or, "Lauren is just overly sensitive."

I couldn't even figure it out for myself most days, and the lack of understanding from others just made me feel more isolated.

Along with depression, and anxiety, often other forms of emotional or mental distress developed. For me, it was a mild form of OCD (Obsessive Compulsive Disorder). It was brought on by stress, but also genetic, as my father has it (although would not admit it). My struggle with OCD was mainly about hand washing. I found myself coming home from school and spending 20 minutes washing my hands. I thought that was bad! Others in the household would get mad at me for my obsessive habits, as if it was by my own choosing. I couldn't control it; at least at first I couldn't! I eventually started going to a Psychiatrist, to try to get to the bottom of my battle with depression, anxiety, and OCD. It took time to really want to go. The first few times, I had to drag myself to go, and almost felt a sense of embarrassment in front of my family. I felt like I was being judged by them, instead of being supported and condoned for not only admitting that I had an issue, but that I actually took the needed steps on the road of recovering from the mental health issue of which the stigma needed so desperately to be relieved.

I found out from my Psychiatrist, that contrary to what my family may have thought at the time, my OCD was actually rather mild. My doctor had said that they had patients whom would spend 3-4 HOURS washing their hands and focusing on other compulsive behaviors. That gave me a new perspective to my own situation. Now for those of you out there who don't like the idea of talking to a stranger about your problems, please remember this: they have a third party, outside opinion, which does bring clarity and new perspective, on top of being a trained professional. I was and still am so proud of myself for dealing with my struggles, and at a young age. There are many people out there who go through most of their lives being stuck in denial, instead of allowing themselves to become a stronger, better version of themselves.

I was prescribed a low-dose of anti-depressants, which I did take for a while, but did not like doing so. I preferred a more natural approach to bettering my health, if possible. There was cognitive therapy which was effective in changing obsessive thoughts and behaviors.

During the process of overcoming "my struggles" was that many days often felt like Groundhog Day. As if every day was all the same, and felt like I was on this treadmill in life. I felt that I was moving, but not really going anywhere. I had to tell myself to just be happy, but I didn't feel happy. I didn't feel joy, or motivated, or inspired. As much as I felt an array of painful emotions, I also felt numb at the same time. In life, we have to live it, so, as to create our own happiness, embrace it, and put ourselves out there for opportunities... but when it comes to the big, bad monsters of depression and anxiety, it doesn't work that way. Some people think that you can just "snap out of it," but it is not so. It can make it hard to get out of bed in the mornings, but is also the very thing that keeps you awake at night.

"It is often in the darkest skies that we see the brightest stars."
~Richard Evans

100

There were days that I wished would just hurry up and end, in the hopes that I would somehow feel better the next day. Then days turning into nights where the anxiety of my never-ending thoughts and worries would creep up even more, leaving me with very vivid dreams and sometimes nightmares. Those vivid visions, which I was told were trying to tell me something; had symbols of some sort, but then trying to uncover the mystery would often leave me with more anxiety. Again, can someone say "vicious cycle"?

It wasn't until my early twenties that things started becoming clear, and a sense of brightness began looming out of that darkness. I gradually became more active in my own life. A sense of motivation, and my inner go-getter was making her way through to shine once again. Most people in my surrounding environment were asleep, while I had been awakening! Several people in my life were stuck in seeing how the situation was before, instead of seeing how it had become, and the progress that was made. They preferred to see me as the little, weak one, and only seeing flaws, rather than seeing the new-found strength I had built from overcoming the long, harrowing, living nightmare.

"There is no despair so absolute as that which comes with the first moments of our first great sorrow. When we have not yet known what it is to have suffered and healed, to have despaired and recovered hope."
~George Eliot

Even over the last few years, there was a long period of time where every time I turned around, something was messed up, and falling apart. A song I basically used as my life's theme song is "Something's Always Wrong" by Toad the Wet Sprocket. I still have had spurts, of depression, and my anxiety can still flare up from time to time, but I have learned to let go of a lot of worries, and expectations, and go with the flow of life. I feel much more at ease, and present a positive attitude and outlook on life, therefore, life has had a better way of responding to me. It has been said that death is not the greatest loss in life. The greatest loss is what dies within us while we live.

For a long time, I thought that I was dying inside, and that feeling lost, sad, lonely, and afraid was gradually killing my soul and causing physical stress on my body. I had unintentionally put up walls; not so much to keep people away, but rather to see who cared enough to tear those walls down, to help, to care. However, it was that path down a very dark, very long, bumpy road which actually lead me to bringing out again the best parts of me, and discovering new aspects about my mind, heart, and personality that I otherwise was blind to before. I see in me even now, that I still have some of those precious traits as I did when I was a child; the wittiness and sense of humor, gentle, mother-hen-like persona. Then, there are other qualities that have developed in me through my never-ending growth and gained wisdom from the hardships that I thought would have caused me a mental or emotional breakdown. As cliché as it may sound, it is so true that what doesn't kill you makes you stronger! They say God gives his hardest battles to his toughest warriors. Well as much as I appreciated the vote of confidence, I often wondered when God would give me a break, as I felt like everything was slipping through my fingers. I was so scared that I would fall back into that same, miserable depressive rut that I was in before, and prayed so hard that it would not happen again. I had made too much progress in my life; emotionally, mentally, with my budding career, with my personal and family relationships, and my personal connection with myself, for it to all turn to dust, or to have to start back at square one all over again.

Since my struggle with depression and anxiety, I have taken many steps to live my life to the fullest in fulfilling the purpose which I was given. Anything worthwhile in life, takes time, consistency, and effort every day, so as to keep moving forward in this journey of life; for it is the journey that is the destination.

Lauren Dickson is an all-around creative, old soul and certified wedding coordinator, as well as being the Associate Manager of Events & Logistics for Canada Fashion Group. Through her own struggles and heartache, she has built self-resiliency and a deeper connection and love for herself. It is through her own experiences and compassionate demeanor that she hopes to impact and inspire others to fight their demons, discover their authentic individuality, and fully embrace life, not just survive it.

Martha Eleftheriou

Finding Me

I grew up in an average home to working-class immigrant parents in the suburbs. My father worked tirelessly at building his business, while my mother's role was to raise my sister and I. Religion was paramount in our family, especially for my mother, as we practiced within a devout faith in a conservative Christian religion. Although my father believed in the teachings of the religion, he chose not to attend or participate in any of the meetings and gatherings for his own reasons.

Being raised in such a devout faith, facilitated a strong spiritual practice of prayer. I learned to pray and say thank you, first and foremost. Even as young as a four-year-old girl, I was thankful and prayed for simple things like food, water and juice. Later, as I grew up, I prayed for just about anything that was bothering me. I prayed for my family, for my mother who experienced many challenges in her life with my physically abusive father and caring for her incurably ill brother. I prayed that my father would stop getting drunk on the weekends and stop physically abusing our family. I prayed for my sister to cope with the emotional impact of witnessing my father's abuse toward me and my mother. I prayed for my cousins and for my friends to strengthen their connection to God. I prayed for myself and for my salvation. I prayed for all of the world to live in peace and harmony the way God had intended it to be. I was as happy and as fulfilled as I possibly could be with that version of spirituality because it granted me refuge from the pain of living in an abusive environment.

As the eldest of two children, I took the brunt of my father's physical and emotional abuse. When I stood up for my mother or my sister and back-talked to my father, he would slap me so hard in the face me, at times, I would fall over. On a family trip to Florida, my younger sister and I were arguing in the backseat of the car, next thing I knew, my father had pulled the car over on the side of the road, in the pouring rain, and lost all control as he unleashed his fury on me. He continuously struck me on my back, my bottom and across the face for what seemed like an eternity to my 7-year-old self. I could do nothing but scream and cry while my family watched in terror with tears from the inside of the car. I had no idea what I had done to deserve this type of treatment as I sat back in the car soaking wet and covered with stinging red marks all over my body. I remember thinking that my father hated me and that I would hate him forever. This episode stayed with me for the rest of my childhood years as he often cited, "Remember what I did to you in Florida?" as a threat before he would physically abuse me again. Being the feisty, strong-willed kid I was, I would talk back and say, "Go ahead, I don't care!" to which the abuse would happen all over again.

The scariest part of the physical abuse was when my father would make me walk straight up to him, knowing I was going to get another stinging slap across the face. I remember shaking in my boots and buckling at the knees as he stood across the kitchen and yelled for me to go up to him to receive my punishment. "Here!" he would bellow and point his index finger to the ground by his feet. I would hesitate from fear and then

I would hear his words again, "HERE NOW!" and very slowly, with tears streaming down my face, I would walk up to him, shaking throughout my body, and face my certain outcome. When I was 12-years-old, my father physically pinned me down and repeatedly hit me across the face and arms. I'll never forget trying my hardest to physically fight back, but just could not wrestle free against his immense physical strength. I promised myself in my diary that night, that when I grew up, my life would never, be anything like the life I was now living.

If I didn't get physically abused for talking back or being out of line, or for any other seeming misbehavior, I regularly heard the words, "shut-up stupid kid." Most times those words prefaced the threat about what would happen to me if I didn't shut up. At a family gathering, my father threatened to physically abuse me at my relatives' home right in front of them. I had been all of 13-years-old. He had been drinking and I could see the anger and aggression in his eyes. My teenage pride took over and the next thing I heard was my own voice yelling at my father in front of all my family, "You fucking asshole!" and I ran. I ran out of the house as fast as my legs could take me down the street and as far away as I could get, because I knew what would happen next.

To my surprise, my father never came after me that day. That's because my uncle had called the police. A family friend who was there came to find me and tell me to come back since the police were waiting to speak to me at the house. The police asked me if I wanted to press charges because of his threats in front of witnesses, but explained that it would be difficult to have him convicted because he hadn't actually assaulted me then and there in front of anyone. I decided that I would not press charges. And from that day, my father did not physically harm me again. He did continue to verbally abuse me and my mother or throw and break plates across the room when he was drunk, but thankfully, the physical abuse stopped when I became a teenager. I don't know if the physical wounds were worse than the emotional wounds or the other way around. What I do know, is that growing up in that household affected my self-worth and my self-esteem. This is why the religion I grew up in provided much comfort and solace. It helped me navigate the demands of growing up with abuse through a strong supportive community of friends and family. If my father couldn't love me for who I was, God surely could. And He did.

I could have easily turned to things such as drinking, drugs and promiscuity feeling so unloved by my father, but instead, I turned to God. Through my spiritual practice of prayer and worship, I carried on and gained the support and divine love of not only God but of the community. What I felt I lacked from my father, I got from the religion. At the same time, I felt extremely disempowered as a child. I felt like there was nothing I could say or do to prevent my father from abusing me or my mother and then, as I grew into my teenage years, I felt disempowered in the religion that had provided so much comfort and hope.

I began questioning why women were not allowed to give sermons from the podium and why they had to wear knee length, or longer, skirts and dresses during times of worship. I wondered why women had to stay silent for the most part and not take on any leadership roles other than in the role of support toward the men in the religion. Participating in extra-curricular activities at school such as clubs and sports teams and pursuing post-secondary education were also frowned upon and discouraged, although not openly banned.

I joined the basketball team in the 9th grade. I really didn't feel there was anything wrong with playing organized sports. I remember praying about it and feeling like God was okay with this decision. My mother, although not overly happy that I was on the team, just said to be careful and to watch that I don't pick up on "bad" habits that would ruin my relationship with God. I received comments from congregation members telling me things like, "you need to be very careful" and don't forget the scripture, "bad associations spoil useful habits." That scripture was repeated to me so many times in my youth that I will never forget it. I wrestled with feelings of guilt, shame and doing something "bad" simply for joining the basketball team although I knew deep down inside, I was not doing anything wrong or bad at all. I questioned myself and what was wrong with me, why I wasn't acting "spiritual" enough or "good" enough and, at times, I believed that I wasn't good enough to receive God's love because I didn't agree with all the rules of "His" religion.

Toward my late teens, the rules did not resonate with me anymore because I began to grasp how they would immensely hold me back from realizing my true personal power. Just as I felt stifled and subjugated as a child in my immediate family, I now began to feel the same way within the religion. Because I felt safe and protected within the confines of the religion, I felt I had nowhere to go but to stay in the religion and swallow whatever issues I disagreed with. I was living in a bubble. The bubble was the religion. I only felt safe and in the right space and place as long as I had my religion. I had the fear of God in me that was for sure, but I also had the fear of being rejected by the community and my family. I knew if I questioned anything, I would be viewed as disobeying God and would be counseled to help straighten out my rebellious thinking. I was taught to believe that if I disobeyed the rules, I would hurt and displease God.

A family friend conducted bible study with me about some of the issues I disagreed upon surrounding sports teams, higher education, and women's rights, or lack thereof. She read scripture after scripture to me proving to me, this was God's will and that, as obedient servants of God, we had to obey. If we didn't obey, we were unfaithful to God we wouldn't be able to gain everlasting life at the end of time. She told me to keep my thoughts to myself and to pray about it.

I felt deflated and small again. I wanted someone to help me out, to let me know that there wasn't anything wrong with me for questioning these beliefs. Instead, I heard the usual advice. I couldn't be who I really was because, I couldn't openly talk about my fears, doubts, and uncertainties. I felt completely suppressed and repressed. I wanted to spread my wings and fly while at the same time crawl into a hole and hide. I just wanted to be loved by God and my family. I wanted to be accepted for who I really was, although, I didn't even know who I was.

At the same time, I began exploring what I wanted to do or become after high school. I had a dream to work with people and help them heal their lives, although I was not yet healed myself. I knew I wanted to pursue university education but, at the same time, struggled with that decision. I knew I would be frowned upon by my religious community simply for going to university. I decided to go anyway. I knew that higher education was the right decision for me, and, somewhere deep down inside my heart, I also knew that educating myself would liberate and empower me.

And then slowly, gradually, something happened. After a few years in university, I began having deep and meaningful conversations with friends who were not a part of my religion. Those interactions and conversations led me to question all the rules, regulations and answers I had believed in so fiercely my entire life. I began to excavate and read a variety of spiritual, philosophical and metaphysical books. All of this type of reading and personal research was definitely not allowed in the religion, but I did it anyway. I began to unlearn everything I had been taught. I questioned my own beliefs and why I held onto these beliefs so strongly.

What I had realized about myself during those early years of my spiritual quest, was that I didn't choose my beliefs. It was ingrained since childhood that these beliefs were the "Truth." Anything contrary to that "Truth," according to them, there would be no way I could be a true servant of God.

By this point in my life, I knew I couldn't be a part of this religion anymore as own beliefs started to form, however, I didn't know where to turn. I gradually stopped attending the meetings. I remember feeling uneasy, that my stability and deep spiritual connection with God would end, as I wasn't practicing spirituality in the only way "I was supposed to." I felt like I had betrayed God, but still stood up for myself at the same time. I felt alone, sad and lost but desired to continue my strong relationship with God. I just had no idea how I would do that without being part of an organized religion with beliefs and rules for worship.

It was one warm summer evening and I distinctly remember a conversation I had with my cousin about my burning desire to find the answers and purpose for my spiritual life. She did her best to console me and explain that I would be happy and fulfilled once I graduated university with my teaching degree, but I really didn't feel that was it. I knew that this journey would take me much deeper than solely through academic achievement. This night, was significant, as I decided, as a 21-year-old young woman, that no matter what I did in my life, I would spend it searching for the spiritual state of elation and peace that I had only experienced during deep states of prayer.

During another conversation with a friend, she recommended I read books by Deepak Chopra. The next day, I headed to the local bookstore to buy one of his books. The book, "How To Know God" would forever change my life. This was exactly what I needed and at precisely the perfect time! As I read it, I felt like God was taking care of me and speaking to me through this book. I came to learn and to believe, that God was not somewhere out there, in heaven, that needed human supplication, but rather, inside of me.

I realized that the strong feeling of peace, support and unconditional love I felt when I prayed existed, because I was connecting to something far greater than myself. I was actually connecting to God and He was and always will be a part of me, regardless of what external practices or actions I partook in. That book was particularly instrumental as the starting point of my spiritual quest, and although my connection to the divine started at a very young age, that pivotal point in my life, during my early 20s, would forever change the trajectory of my life.

For the first time in my life, I began to make decisions based on what I felt was right and wrong in my heart, instead of looking for answers from outside of myself. Most importantly, I began to feel divinely supported and loved regardless of what my spiritual practice looked like. I realized that although I didn't have all the answers, I would be alright because I still had my connection to God. My connection was different but a connection nonetheless. I still prayed daily and through praying, I felt a comfort and peace within my heart that everything would work out for me.

The process of forgiving my father for what he had done to me as a child wasn't an easy one. I wanted to be free. Free from pain and blame and to let go of the past. During a self-help course I was taking at the time, one of the exercises for healing the past was to call the person who had deeply hurt you and say I love you to them. I called my father and hesitantly said, "I love you, dad." I heard nothing but silence on the phone before he replied, "Martha, what kind of silly course are you taking?" but then after a few seconds replied, "I love you too, my girl." This was a huge shift in my healing process with my father as we rarely said I love you to each other. And I believed him. I realized that he did love me even though he hurt me. Many years later, when I came to learn about his own terrible childhood with physical abuse, I understood why he was the way he was.

The quest for purpose, fulfillment, freedom, personal empowerment and inner peace had begun. I made it my mission to stay the course until I felt it from my heart and soul. Regular yoga practice helped strengthen my connection to the divine and my inner self. A few years later, I met and eventually married my soul and life partner, Michael.

My husband and I decided to attend a meditation and yoga retreat one summer a few years after we were married. An intuitive feeling spoke to my heart and let me know that this one week together, fully immersed in our spiritual journey would forever change us. And that it did! During that week, we learned how to meditate, we deepened our spiritual connection to all that is and to one another. Upon a chance encounter in the elevator with the retreat's yoga teacher, she suggested I become a yoga teacher. I chuckled it off as a lovely compliment. Although I loved yoga, I had no interest in teaching it. After we returned from the retreat we felt on top of the world and to our surprise, we found ourselves pregnant with our first child after that month!

Fast forward nine months— we welcomed our first child into the world. I couldn't have been any happier but within a few days after giving birth and bringing our daughter home, a strange, awkward and completely unwanted feeling of desperation and desolation came to visit and stayed with me for about six weeks. I had no idea what this feeling was, as I had never experienced anything remotely like this before! I was completely in love with my baby and distraught at the life I had left behind both at the same time. I realized after the first few months of becoming a new mom, that I experienced intense baby blues.

After the first two years of motherhood, I felt like I had lost myself. Here I was, feeling like I should be on top of the world with my life, but instead I was feeling lost, scared, alone and disempowered. The feelings I knew too well from my childhood and youth. Everything I felt I had worked so hard to overcome, seemed to have resurfaced. Although I still practiced yoga, I felt like I didn't know who I really was or who I wanted to be. I went back to work part-time as a school teacher so that I could spend more time with my daughter; however, there was a yearning and a stirring which started to happen from somewhere deep down in my soul that was calling me to search for more, to search for myself and to find my place in the world.

One evening at a yoga class, my mentor and teacher, Faith, mentioned there was a yoga teacher training program beginning at the studio. I recalled the chance encounter with the yoga teacher three-years prior at the retreat, who randomly mentioned I should teach yoga. "Could this be for me? Should I take this program?" I wondered to myself. I had made up my mind. This is what I would pursue for the next six months of my life. I experienced a huge personal shift not only spiritually, but also, with the forgiveness work toward my father during that time.

One significant experience that will forever be etched into my heart and soul, had been during a particular yoga nidra class. Time suddenly came to a stand-still and I had my life-altering spiritual a-ha moment. Words cannot truly justify the feelings and the pure magnificence of what I encountered. As I lay there and listened to Faith's voice guide me into relaxing my body, one part at a time, I let go of my thoughts and and felt myself surrendering to the silence and stillness of the present moment.

Somewhere toward the end of the class, like an unexpected thunderous clap in the sky, my heart, mind, body and soul remembered! I remembered who I really was and what I was doing here in this lifetime. I remembered that I was a divine child of God or source or the divine or the universe, (by this point I had detached from the specific word God as I came to believe that no human word could describe the true nature and essence of this consciousness) and that, not only was I this perfect spiritual child completely deserving of love, but that I was an extension of the divine experiencing itself as me. I felt tears of joy, sadness, relief, and appreciation stream down my cheeks. I cried for the little girl inside of me who felt unloved by her father. I cried for the little girl who feared breaking the rules and being rejected by God and her community. Mostly, I cried because I now felt free! Fully free from all of the pain hiding deep within my cells and free to love myself for who I really was. I felt my soul finally break free because I knew, felt and experienced myself for who and what I really was... a spiritual extension of the divine, having a human experience!

After that, I was completely bewildered and in a state of disbelief. What the heck was that? As much as my ego wanted to tell me it was utterly made up and just a fiction of my vivid imagination, I knew otherwise. With every fiber of my being, I knew I had just experienced total oneness and connection with God and, although I was in a state of shock, I knew it was real.

I got home that night and tried my best to relay my experience to my husband, and although he did his best to listen, he couldn't really comprehend what I had just undergone. I felt an immense connection to unconditional divine love... what I had yearned for my entire life! I was vigorously searching during the past two decades of my life to understand who I was, why I had to go through what I went through as a child, and what I was supposed to do while on this planet with this life given to me, and now I knew. I had no idea how I would share this spiritual understanding with the world, but I knew I would. I trusted that I had been divinely guided and directed with every event in my life to this point in time, and I had a strong conviction that the universe would not let me down... it never had!

With this understanding of who I really was, I sought further spiritual guidance and healing through various healers and mentors. One such occasion, after an energy healing session, the healer passed on a very important message to me from my father, who is still alive. She told me she heard a message from his soul and the message were the words "I'm sorry" repeated three times. Like my experience with connecting to the divine,

I knew this was real. My father knew how deeply he had hurt me and was now sending me a message energetically to let me know he was remorseful. I couldn't help but cry tears of joy and pain because I had longed to hear those words from his mouth all those years, but I never did. It didn't matter whether I actually heard those words from my father's mouth or in this energetic form. I decided to fully accept his apology and to begin a new and different relationship with him.

Since that spiritual awakening all those years ago, I've pursued continued spiritual opening and awareness through receiving my spiritual life coaching certification, becoming a Reiki master and through teaching yoga. All of these modalities have helped me to heal myself from the wounds of my abusive childhood and controlling religion. But what I'm most grateful for, is that I have learned to love myself and to accept myself as a beautiful and complete child of God just for being who I am! I know who I am and I know I am loved and accepted by God just because I am alive! I don't need to prove myself to anyone or anything. I just need to be ME!

Today, my spiritual practice is very simple. I spend time alone in nature. I make time for silence, stillness and personal reflection and connection to the universe through both prayer and meditation. I practice and teach yoga. I practice gratitude every morning and every evening before I go to bed. When I partake in these activities, I am filled up and re-fueled spiritually. I am reminded that I am never alone and that I am always divinely supported.

I am grateful for all of the experiences I have had in my life thus far, nothing has been in vain. I value every single experience, whether pleasant or painful, happy or sad, easy or difficult as they all have led to me where I am today.

Through the many years of healing and spiritual growth, I have forgiven my father. I understand that his own childhood pain and abuse were responsible for my pain and abuse, and, although this awareness does not justify the way he treated me, I understand it. Unhealed past pain leads to further future pain.

The beauty of finding myself through my spiritual journey has enabled me to see the blessings and find the lessons. I am grateful for the religion of my youth, for it taught me, through the contrast of control and obedience, how to question and think for myself and how to decide what is right or wrong for me! I learned to use my heart as my guide when making decisions. With my heart leading my journey, I have found my own personal power through liberation of the past. Despite feeling broken and lost during the early years of my spiritual quest, God never abandoned me because I came to understand that God resides in the temple of my heart. I have remembered who I am, what I have come here to do, and that I was, all along, whole and complete in oneness with God.

Martha Eleftheriou is a Women's Empowerment and Spiritual Life Coach, Writer, Motivational Speaker, Reiki Master and Yoga Teacher (RYT). She works with women of all ages to help them uncover their dreams and purpose in order to live their lives with passion and fun. She loves reading, writing and taking regular nature walks. She lives with her husband and two daughters in King City, Ontario, Canada.

Perspective

What you think, you become.
What you feel, you attract.
What you imagine, you create.
- Buddha

Life. It's wild. It's bright. It's dark. It's fun. It's funny. It's hard. It's wonderful. It's unbearable. It's all of these things, sometimes at the same time and it changes constantly. If you are lucky enough and interested enough to explore and embrace it fully, you will be a wiser, calmer, humble, and more open-minded individual, experienced with the knowledge that endless possibilities exist for you to create the life you want and an overwhelming number of opportunities to share the gifts you have.

My life isn't perfect, but my perception of it is. That is, it's perfect for me. As I reflect on how I have gotten to this point in my life, I am overwhelmed with gratitude and proud of the path I have taken to get here. Looking back, I see how the seemingly unexpected opportunities that came my way, were actually harnessed by life decisions I had made and the energy (skills, talents, interests, relationships, growth and synergy with the universe) that I created through those experiences. Today, I aim to live with the intention to create joy, happiness and fulfillment for myself and then share that abundance with others. This, I believe, is the purpose of life.

People are intrinsically meant to be happy and I believe happiness is a choice. When you do find yourself unhappy or unfulfilled— which you will at times throughout your life, you (alone) have the power change your course. What I have learned is that happiness comes from within and incredible personal and professional opportunities present themselves when you are living as closely fulfilled to happiness as possible.

What does that mean, exactly? Don't we all want to, strive to, hope to be happy? Surely, we do, but life, things we cannot control, other people's opinions, they all get in the way. Disappointments, Failures, Rejections, they all get in the way. Or do they? Perhaps, if you alter your perception, you might see, that these things have instead, cleared the way.

Let's talk about change. It is a constant. Situations, jobs, homes, and people change. Everything changes, just like the weather and the sooner you learn to embrace the rain, the hail, the snow, the sleet and the sunshine— especially on days when the weatherman got it wrong— the closer you will be to understanding that perception is everything and happiness is your choice to make, regardless of anything else.

So while we can not control the weather, we can certainly weather the storm any way we like. I choose to take control of my course with optimism and adventure and only now, looking back, I realize I always have.

Think about the timespan of your life as one of those fun puzzles you played when you were a kid, (I have three kids, so I see these puzzles on the back of every kid's meal at every restaurant). Picture the maze where you navigate with a pencil from the starting point to the ending point trying to avoid the dead ends. If you think about this maze as your journey through life, you can see that we each have the same goal to embark upon, which is to travel through from beginning to end. We essentially "start" at birth, each with a different set of unique circumstances, of course, but with a journey ahead of us and choices to be made along the way.

Consider that first major bend in your maze of life. This is the point in your life where you have made some critical decision on your own. For some, that age is younger, for others, older. For some, that decision is forced upon you, and for others, it is a privilege or an opportunity to do something life changing.

For me, this first bend in the maze of life occurred when I was 20 years old. As a child, I lived where I lived and went with the flow of decisions that were made for me. I grew up a generally happy, optimistic and resilient child with parents who loved me and introduced me to travel at a young age. I was quiet when I was young. Not shy, just reserved. I wouldn't say I was highly focused or knew what I wanted to do when I grew up. I wouldn't say I knew what kind of woman I would become and I certainly wouldn't say I ever thought, growing up a quiet and reserved girl, that I would become so vocal around the things I deem to be important in life which is the pursuit of happiness and the empowerment for women.

The big bend in my maze was the first of many that opened my eyes wide, and my heart even wider. My decision and subsequent experience set my course of life on a trajectory of open-mindedness, adventure, self-reliance and growth. When I was 20 years old, I sailed around the world through a study abroad program called Semester at Sea. I didn't know it then, when I filled out the paper application, that this decision would lead me on a journey of self-discovery that would widen my perspective of the world, and the place I fit in it, so greatly, that it essentially erased any potential "dead-ends" in the maze of life I was navigating through. Ah, perspective... it is everything, as I have come to learn.

Living on a ship, stopping to explore life in other countries is a diverse, vivid and humbling experience. It is sensory overload and emotionally overwhelming to go to bed one day in Africa and wake up the next in India. The smells, the sounds, the sights and the livelihood of each country are so drastically different and extremely extreme.

My intention was to fully immerse myself and be present each day with my thoughts, feelings and actions. I didn't want to just "see" the world from my reserved and quiet perspective, I wanted to feel the world and live it without reservation. Like a butterfly emerging from the safety of the cocoon, I felt myself spreading my wings and becoming more of the woman I wanted to be. Specifically, I became less quiet with my thoughts and feelings. I put myself out there, sharing more of who I am with others. I became more inquisitive with those around me, in a way I had never been before. My curiosity wasn't about where people were from or what they studied or how they lived. I wanted to know people in a more profound way. What made them happy? What made their spirits soar?

What I experienced in 100 days around the world and the way I embraced it in my heart was altogether empowering and life-changing. My maze of life has been on a wild, winding puzzle pattern ever since. Up, down and all around, just like the journey of my travels and the wide range of emotions my journey has taken me through along the way. High on life one minute, low from the harsh realities of living the next. Change is constant and life is complex. Happiness, I found, despite this, is still available in abundance, through perspective and gratitude.

Humility, Gratitude, Happiness... they are just some of the emotions I felt while traveling... many times simultaneously. Learning to live in the moment is something I cherish now and it has helped me live my life in a genuine way.

Your whole perspective changes when you see things like children bathing in a rusty tub of dirty water, next to a make-shift stall covered in pieces of tin and tarp. This stall sold goats — dead ones, hanging from a tattered rope, with blood dripping down their necks by men that appeared to be blind. The film on their eyes made their eye color more blue that black against their brown skin and I wondered how anyone could live in these conditions. I tried not to exude pity or shock as I walked through this shanty village in South Africa. I was conscious of my energy and I didn't want it to express anything but kindness. My simple presence was an intrusion enough, I am sure. Have you ever just tried to look someone in the eyes without judging the world around them? It's a beautiful thing.

Later that same afternoon, I enjoyed a meal and a cocktail in an upscale and expensive restaurant on the Cape Town Harbour overlooking penguins on the beach. I felt torn and guilty. Why was my meal so expensive? Why did I get enjoy it? Why do some lack opportunities to live in way that I take for granted?

The dichotomy of wealth and color that exists within miles of each other there, and in many other places around the world, feels unfair and downright wrong. I met Archbishop Desmond Tutu during that trip, he was a bright and brilliant ray of light with his smile and his energy. I was happy to meet him, I was humbled by my experience and I was grateful for people like him that fight for the rights of others. I was deeply inspired.

Inspiration is everywhere. I found it in rainforests and water-falls in Venezuela. Excitement is all around us and it was thrilling on the streets of Brazil during Carnival and breathtaking on the back of a safari truck watching a lioness with her cubs in Nairobi. Humility exits when you humble yourself and I felt it as I took my shoes off and placed them amongst the thousands of others on the cold marble of the Taj Mahal. Joy is but a fleeting moment, but when it's there, you should embrace it, and I did, laughing wildly on the back of a moped in Saigon. Gratitude is gift and I closed my eyes on a deserted beach under the bright moonlight in Malaysia and gave thanks.

The wonders of this world are beautiful to see, but as I learned, they are simultaneously interwoven with the harsh realities of the human experience. Over dinner in Brazil, a tiny homeless boy was punched in the thin stomach by a police officer because he was begging for food at my table. Hungry and maimed children hung from my arms in the streets of India, following me for miles, it seemed, begging for coins and calling me Aunty. The abandoned but perhaps luckier, handicapped children lay in an orphanage. They are incapable of begging, but at least have a roof over their head and food to eat. On a train going to Agra, I was glared at by men, a lot of them, crammed in the heat. The blatant, unflinching glares looked a lot like anger, but felt more like curiosity. I have no idea, but it was scary. Vietnam was hot, hotter than anywhere else, underground in a tunnel, one that was pitch black and only small enough to crawl through as I learned many lived like this for weeks and months on end, during the Vietnam War. I picked up a postcard of a young girl aiming a rifle in a field and she looked like me. On a bus in Japan, a man was laughing so hard and hysterically, he couldn't stop. It was so peculiar it had my friends and I laughing too. At what, we didn't know. I learned later that the atomic bomb dropped in Hiroshima disintegrated those in it's wake immediately, and had lasting mental and physical effects on those in the womb of mother's miles and miles away from where it detonated.

The juxtaposition between that which is wonderful and that which is woeful is an interesting phenomenon. They say in order to fully experience happiness, you must experience sorrow. It's yin and yang and must exist in the same space in order to appreciate it. This is an important lesson and an empowering one. If you can can embrace the highs and lows of life, you can better control your perspective about them. The highs in life are awesome and you should celebrate them every single chance you get, knowing that perhaps the moment is fleeting and can change almost as quickly as it arrived. The lows are never as bad they seem, especially if you have a grander perspective of life and have seen that your low, isn't as low as someone else's. Everything changes constantly and situations are temporary. The good exists with the bad and they are what they are— it's how you deal with them that will affect your spirit. Can you soften your heart in the wake of that which breaks your heart? Can you become less judgmental when you see that which make you want to judge? Can you find happiness in places it doesn't seem to exist? Yes, you can, and you should.

When you realize you create your own happiness, the world has endless opportunities. Your positive energy attracts new and exciting opportunities to take advantage of— you just have to embrace life for all that it is and chose a positive perspective in spite of it.

My love for adventure, took me to to Bangkok, Thailand in May of 2000. I taught English at a university and took a side job editing at a local newspaper station. I explored the city by boat, motorbike, train, taxi and tuk-tuk. I walked through the markets, districts, stadiums and temples and I traveled on my time off to other countries- Cambodia, Vietnam, China the Philippines, Nepal and Italy. Again, I saw the highs and I experienced the lows. Angkor Wat is one of the most beautiful and historical wonders of the world. Located in Phnom Penh, not too far from the killing fields of Cambodia- where human skulls are displayed in a shrine, outside of an old school turned torture camp, from the 1970's. Blood stains are still visible, splattered on the walls and ceilings. It was a museum of sorts, but not like the kind we have in Washington, DC where every- thing is sterile and neatly documented to read. This museum was sad and seemingly abandoned, just like the people were when the war was over and the devastation remained. I saw a little girl carrying a heavy melon on her head, standing outside of what looked to be a brothel. I smiled at her and she smiled back with her mouth, but had despair and deep sadness in her eyes. That vision still brings tears to my eyes and an ache in my heart to this day. I can hardly share the story without filling up with tears. I didn't have to know her to know her sorrow. I felt it. The feeling has never left me.

I took a trip alone that year to Nepal. In Kathmandu, I arrived late at night, but the streets were so alive and vibrant, it felt like the middle of the day. People are everywhere, selling things, eating things, sitting around, just connecting. It was so busy, there was no need to scared. It was colder than I expected, so I bought a North Fase coat. Yes, Fase with an "s", from a little girl and her stall/shop/home. She spoke English, so we chatted, she wanted to braid my hair so I let her and then she showed me her home, behind the stall. It was a one room area, with mats and pots and pans and her family inside. They smiled and they were kind to me. We didn't speak the same language, but we felt the same thing- a genuine warm connection. Later that first night, a little boy asked me to buy something for him at the grocery store. "Formula, for my baby brother." So I did... even as the checkout clerk nodded no, and told me I was being tricked, he'll return it for the money, he said. Which was fine, I didn't mind. Happy to buy it, either way. I found a hostel, spent the night and explored the city the next day by foot. I saw temples, squares, bright colored flags, Hindu priests, a lot of smiling faces and a lot of monkeys- they're everywhere. A few days later, I left Kathmandu to explore a mountainside village a few hours away. On the bus packed with people, luggage and animals I sat next to a young woman, in her twenties like me. She was traveling with her family and spoke English. She told me she was attending medical school- I was impressed! I told her I was traveling the world and she was impressed! Mainly because I was all alone with no man watching out for me.

I got off hours later near a base camp for hikers planning to climb Mt. Everest. I began a hike up a small mountain where no cars can go and no path clearly laid out. It took me about 3 hours to get to the little village at the top. My Fodor's guidebook told me there would be a hostel with a room to rent when I got there -luckily, it was accurate. I stayed in a village called Sarangkot for a few days and it was beautiful, overlooking a Tibetan refugee camp. During those three days I mostly talked to children- boys, because in this remote village, girls did not go to school, or speak English. They walked me around and showed me the different dwellings where they lived, where the water well was, and mainly, they wanted to practice their English. They were curious where I was from, what I was doing there and what was going on with Bill Clinton and Monica Lewinsky-evidently, that was all the rage on the one transistor radio in the village where the villagers got their news. That was unexpected and amusing.

My experience in Nepal taught me one of the most valuable lessons I have ever learned in life, which is: Learning to be alone, but not be lonely. That phrase brings a smile to my face, just writing it because it's so empowering.

Throughout my life, I have come to value this ability tremendously and it also validates my core belief- that happiness comes from within and nowhere else. You create your happiness by decisions you make for yourself and if you don't like something, change your perspective about it and then change your direction.

The maze of my life, just like the winding path up that mountain, was created by me, step by step with adventure in my heart and an open-mindedness about what I would find. The act of finding that which made me the happiest has always been my guide.

While I spent much of my year in Thailand alone, learning how not be lonely, I still am a highly social individual. Throughout my life, I have had plenty of help along the way. There has been plenty of advice sought and advice given. I have leaned on friends and family to get me through things and I enjoy company and often being the center of it. What I know, in my heart, though, is that I don't need anything from another person to find joy in life.

I can create it on my own and I can share it, which makes that joy multiply.

By the end of my year in Thailand, I felt empowered by my travels and confident in myself as a brave and independent woman. Yet, this feeling was not without the contrasting feeling I already came to understand about the human experience. Yin and Yang. When one thing exists, the opposite must also exist. What I felt so deeply though my independence, was the lack of freedom for so many others. While I maneuvered around the earth freely exploring, observing and experiencing, many and mostly women were not. While I felt empowered, many felt despair and I could see it their eyes and feel it in their presence. No matter where I was in the world, including my own backyard, the plight women have for opportunity, education and basic equality exists.

This universal truth is one that has affected me greatly. It's more than an observation or an understanding about history and the way the world works. Travel has changed me in so many ways. Historical accounts in textbooks came alive for me not exactly when I was climbing the steps at the Great Wall, but when I sat with an elderly woman, on the stoop of her door nearby as she showed me the old shoes she was selling. They looked like ballet slippers, pointed and tiny and then I looked at her feet, they were pointed and tiny like her shoes. In her time and her culture foot-binding was a practice that made a woman more attractive and increased her marriage potential. She was a sweet woman and I wondered what her life had been like growing up a young girl in China, having to bind her feet in a painful way day after day, year after year. In Bangkok, I enjoyed many ceremonies with traditional dancing and customs. I was already educated about their history and love for their King, but I went to spa to get a massage, and was told to select my masseuse from the twenty young ladies behind the glass window smiling and wearing the same tight dress, I felt shame being there and I felt their shame for being there too, behind the glass. Experiences like this changed me and the plight of women around the world has become a circumstance that I can't ignore. It has become a strong calling to use my voice to advocate for the empowerment of women— all women and all girls, everywhere.

As a wife and mother, as a woman who was once a little girl and as person who traveled the world, leading not as a female in the sense of her limitations but as a capable individual, with the ability to blend in anywhere- I have developed the trait of relating with just about anyone. I feel a connection with women, regardless of their background, and I have a strong sense that their situation could easily be mine and vise versa. I have reached a point in my life where the compassion I have felt for unfair circumstances women are put into have been met with a calm confidence to do something about it. It's my calling.

What I know is that the spot in which our maze of life starts, has everything to do with where we are born, and what we are born into. We all have opportunities to make decisions, some decisions easier than others and some so hard, many of us will never have to make them. Yet, we all still have a journey through life to make and the opportunity to embrace the ups and downs, choosing a positive perspective to move us forward. While I truly believe happiness is choice and we alone can choose the path to happiness, I also know that compassion, inspiration and advocacy for others is powerful and moving. Literally, I aim to create action and increase awareness and to galvanize women to see their full potential, harness happiness from within and create the life they want to lead.

In 2015, I entered a state pageant and won the title of Mrs. DC America. I had never been in a pageant before, nor was it something I ever wanted to do. The opportunity seemed to come out of nowhere... or did it? The year was phenomenal. It was empowering and exciting and glamorous and fun. It was everything I love about the things I love to pursue- different, challenging, and with the opportunity to grow. At the national Mrs. America Pageant in Las Vegas, I placed in the semi-finals and finished in the Top15. I wasn't the prettiest, most fit, most prepared and definitely not the tallest woman there. We were all uniquely beautiful, poised and very prepared on that stage. What I was, was proud, passionate and positive. I was proud to represent Washington, DC, a city that I loved and meant more to me than ever because it's where I met the love of my life, and where my three other loves were born. I was beaming with pride to be married to my husband- who is handsome, humble and incredibly supportive. I spoke passionately about my platform— The Empowerment of Women through Entre-preneurship, and I approached every woman I met there with positivity and friendship. I did not win the crown or title of Mrs. America that year. I did win a year of excitement and lifetime of new friendships.

I put forth a tremendous amount of effort that year being a community advocate and championing for my platform. I volunteered often and included my children every chance I could. I grew as person and challenged myself in ways I never had before. I'm so grateful for the opportunity to have served as Mrs. DC America 2015 and I hope I inspired other women to present her best self and pursue her dreams, whatever they may be. I always say, "The modern, married woman can and should have it all, whatever "all" means to her."

As I follow the path I have made through my maze of life so far, I feel an overwhelming sense of gratitude. I love my place in the world today and while life isn't always perfect, I am always empowered. I am purposefully positive and positively fulfilled. I am inspired to do more, be more and give more. And my journey continues.

Elaine Espinola is a speaker, spokesperson and entrepreneur. An on-air personality, Elaine is the host of a local television show for Comcast Cable and the national podcast host for the Better Business Bureau. Elaine's love for travel has led to adventures all over world and her passion for strong female leadership earned her title of Mrs. DC America, 2015. Elaine is an anti-human trafficking advocate and strong voice for the empowerment of women, everywhere.

Pina Ferraro

The Me I Didn't Know

There I was, at 3:00 a.m. in the still of darkness, at the mercy of yet another sleepless night my head full of the not so planned trip down memory lane. The painful memories held their place in my already broken self, every emotion tied me to another chain of unexpected events in my life. Every bruise began to show the downward spiral I had been thrown into, holding myself and rocking myself back and forth with the hopes of feeling comforted. The haunting memories kept me lost and confused. My hands were shaking and my throat felt tight as I was unable to swallow. The dryness in my mouth made it difficult for me to utter a sound. This feeling of desperation came over me, having the need to call out to someone, anyone, but in the late hours of the night as my son slept soundly in the next room. I was prisoner in this state.

I tried to calm myself down. Scared to the very core of my being, I was unaware of how to control what was happening to me. I walked around my apartment nervously, pacing back and forth. I then sat on the floor and continued to rock myself back and forth again, but this feeling would not go away.

I took a picture of my beloved mother from the mantel, held it tightly to my chest. As I laid there on the floor crying out to her, I begged her to help me understand why this sadness pushed me into this unfamiliar state. These emotions caused me to cry and lose my ability to breathe. I just wanted her to tell me that I was going to be ok, but the memories held my attention to the many circumstances that knocked me down year after year— to every loss I had suffered, every person that had betrayed me forced me into this state.

All the relationships that I held dear to my heart suddenly ended. I was forced to accept the many doors that had closed without any warning or explanations. It was all imploding, sending me into this endless emotional hell. There, with all my shattered pieces along life's road, I laid there scattered, with each piece of me holding their own significance to the devastation. I was once whole with a dream of having a happy every after kind of life, with a bright outlook on all the possibilities, to now... helplessly watching it all unravel.

The life I once knew and planned for, would be forever changed along with the many pieces of my unrecognizable self. I had no idea as to how I would survive or if I would ever come to know this person that has been broken and forever changed.

As I staggered through life, trying to maintain some normalcy, my emotions kept me connected to the past. All the hurt I had endured quietly, and in the midst of asking myself why was this continuing, I was forced to accept that my short lived marriage had to come to an end, the toll it was taking on my son and myself made me realize this was not the life we deserve.

In that split second I made the choice to accept the marriage had to come to a painful and bitter end. I was also dealing with the death of my beloved mother, and the ongoing stress was just too much to pretend I was handling things.

I felt I was fooling everyone around me. The shame I carried inside of me, along with the feeling that I failed as a wife and mother allowed me to stay hidden in this façade acting like I was handling my situation and coping with the reality of raising my son alone. I was now a single parent. However, my evenings became the reality of me unveiling, my true self. The pain that I hid, began to consume me and the mask I wore, fell off. There in my own silent hell, I completely fell apart. I was blinded by how consumed I was, as the pain in the pit of my stomach was unbearable. I felt like I was falling into a bottomless pit and I couldn't get out no matter how hard I tried. There I was, falling further into this sense helplessness. Yet, I was determined to pull myself out, because this was not how I would live.

I found myself on the floor again confused as to how I got there, crying uncontrollably. My fist tightened, as I laid there in a fetal position, praying for God to help me, as the rage inside me became more intense, I was telling myself to stop thinking I was not good enough, stop feeling lost and desperate laying there in this pitiful state. This is not who I am, I don't surrender to a state of defeat. Suddenly the crying stopped and I felt a glimmer of hope and knew I wasn't about to give up on myself.

As I began to recount the endless nights of crying and questioning, how did I get here to this point in my life? When the hell did I lose my way? Why were these circumstances continuing to happen to me? I knew my life was more than just pain and suffering, I knew my life had meaning and purpose.

I was a daughter to a beautiful sensitive woman. I was a devoted wife and partner and loyal and protective mother. Now I sit here with this unfamiliar person that I have now become, whose world has fallen apart. This is not who I am, this is not who I want to be, there is still much more of me to know. Seeing myself as a motherless daughter, a single mother, to a brave little boy, came the responsibility of inheriting these roles and being both mother and father did not come without a lonely price.

My time was now learning how to be a parent again, having to be both sensitive and strong. These two very different emotions that at that very moment in my life, did not exist because of the confusion that surrounded me as to how was I going to gain my footing in this new role. I thought maybe I should start by having just a little faith in myself, believe that I have the ability to maintain some sense of strength and know that no matter if I don't get it right, then I would get up and try again and that would be ok.

As my life continued to play out without my mom and the marriage, there was a glimmer of inspiration as to the reality of life. The important things and people we take for granted, the time we think we have all the tomorrows, taken from us in a blink of an eye, without warning. Time strips us of the many chances we are given to reach out. It also has taught me that we must cherish the moments and the people in our lives, grab hold, of all the endless possibilities that life has to offer us. I had to painfully come to face, that my time with my mother was cut too short. My mom would never be here to see me get to know the woman I have grown into. My mom won't get to see my son grow up and become the man he is meant to become. She won't be at his wedding or see him become a father. She won't be witness to the life I have created for my son and myself.

All these thoughts, still haunt me to this day. How my life is so completely empty and me feeling dead inside because the loss was bigger than I could handle. I carried this with me without sharing it with my family. The daunting reality that I was half of the person I was before mom died. I knew mom would want me to try and live the life I was meant to live. The inner child inside of me still calls out to her in my time of need and uncertainty, when I feel alone and scared. I look to mom for some sense of guidance and comfort. I now live with the devastating memory of when I got the call from my now absent brother, how he told me mom was diagnosed with stage 4 pancreatic cancer, and the doctors didn't give her much time. As the memory played out to the emotions that enraged in me, how I felt alone, not my mother, this isn't fair, she didn't deserve this, she had already sacrificed so much of her own life that this is now how her story end. Why?

I sat there letting the words register within me and again I was hit with these chains of emotions, my breathing became shallow and I started shaking. The heaviness in my chest, the excruciating pain that mom was dying and our time would be cut short. I was in shock and didn't want to believe that this was happening.

I sat selfishly crying thinking about my situation. I whispered to myself, not mom. Not my beautiful mother, how am I supposed to handle what I am going through without her support? She is the glue that held the family together and now my life is starting to fall apart again. I knew I was drowning without mom, because I depended on her, this loving soul that gave me life. The ache and emptiness I felt inside was overwhelming I became locked in this state of despair, my reality that I would never again see mom was too much to endure.

I sat sadly realizing I would never again hear her soft voice, hear the sweet sound of her laughter. I will never feel her arms around me when we'd exchange hugs. I will never get to tell her I love her or hear those words from her again. I will never get to taste her cooking or smell the freshly brewed espresso she loved to have in the early morning rise. I wouldn't get to have our talks out on our porch where we so often did. And in the middle of this painful reality, laid that little girl who so desperately wanted and needed her mother and prayed this nightmare was not happening. For it was only in my lonely hours that I felt trapped with the memories that I turned to prayer to help me through this ordeal.

There I was allowing myself to completely fall apart and try to regain some sense of control and understanding, but I was helpless to what was causing me to become weak and lose my ability to maintain some strength and sense of self. I was exhausted from the endless nights of crying myself to sleep, reliving the past. I was drowning unable to stop the ache and emptiness that was holding me captive. I became confused as to why in such a short period of time, did I have to suffer the loss of my marriage, and now my mother. What was the lesson here? Did I cause this to happen to me? Was this my reality, my destiny, my life? Angry, I refused to give into these negative thoughts and how they were making me think. I would not become victim to my own inability to get past all this and be hopeful.

Every pain tied me a sense of abandonment. Alone, I was trapped in this body that I did not recognise. I wanted so desperately to break free from the chains I felt were holding me down. The chains that kept me tied in this constant whirlwind of memories. I knew I had to pray for some peace throughout all of this, but that would mean I had to accept that my mother was really gone. I had to face the harsh fact that this was now my new reality and somehow I had to find a way to just live. I knew I couldn't go on much longer like this and decided to seek a professional to help with all the stress that I was living with.

I searched around and found a good therapist who was very instrumental in making me become more aware that what I was experiencing was in fact very normal. My therapist didn't feel I was having an emotional breakdown rather that I was experiencing some traumatic stress and would help me find some coping techniques. She mentioned some breathing exercises and meditation to help quiet my mind. I explained every time I closed my eyes, I relived all the suffering I went through during my marriage, the loss of my mother and coping with my son's constant crying every night asking where my mother was. That was most painful of it all. I just wanted to scream why us, why was this happening to my little boy, he had endured so much already with his dad walking out on us. As the therapist help me better explain this all to my son, I felt some sense of peace knowing that I was helping my son better cope with our situation. There are times that I still feel the rage inside of me, wanting to break out into a scream, wishing my mother to still be here and for me to tell her one last time that she is and will always be my life, my home, and that I am because of her, becoming a stronger more determined woman.

The one thing through all my endless, undeniable pain and suffering, is that I understand that no matter the pain, no matter the struggle, your inner ability to pull yourself out of despair is possible and the valuable lessons that are attained are priceless. I love you, mom, and you will always live in my heart. I will continue striving to be the daughter and mother you would want me to be. I know that deep inside me, is that will of determination to continue on through life and believe in myself, for I am far more then that which has happened to me. Out of the emotions of hitting rock bottom, I picked myself up, refusing to stay down, because of my son and myself. For when I look, to the beautiful butterflies that surround me, I will be reminded that you are still here with me. I will look up to the skies and feel the pride within me knowing that I have survived a past of pain and suffering, that little girl inside, that was once broken at a time when she was just starting out in life, who got knocked down— has taken her shattered pieces and rebuilt herself into a woman who emerged more empowered and authentic, loving herself back to life, with confidence,

I look around and see my life as for the first time since I have healed. I now know that I am stronger than my struggles or my pain, and should my past call upon me every now and then, I will smile back with pride and see the road I traveled with all the devastation I overcame. I know that deep within me, I have this inner ability to pull myself out of despair. My past with all my pain, suffering and losses, gave me far more than it could of ever have taken.

The memory of my mother will always be my driving force to live a life she would be proud of and be the mother she would expect me to be. Mom, I will always look to you, as my compass whenever I may feel lost. I will forever be reminded, of our life together, and my journey home, to the me that has grown.

Pina Ferraro is a 15-year breast cancer survivor and a proud mother of a 25-year-old son, who was instrumental in Pina's will to live and over come her cancer as well as her loving family who support carried her to wellness. Pina lives her life full of gratitude and knows how blessed she is and lives her life true to her authentic self and hopes to touch those who know her with love laughter and hope for all of our tomorrow's.

Jen Hecht

The Last Mile

The sun is relentlessly beaming down on the tennis court, not a cloud in the sky for forgiveness from the oppressive heat and humidity. It's August in Michigan. Suicide drills again... every day after an 8-hour tennis camp. I can still remember pressing my fingers down hard on the edge of the double's line and how the heat from the asphalt burns my fingertips. Below is a glimpse of one day of tennis camp leading up to the last mile.

His voice booms throughout the court, "You've all worked so hard today, but now it's time for the worst minute of your life. Don't touch the line, keep your fingers away." I adjust my feet in sprint mode. I have more power on my left side, so I adjust my right foot for support. My ankle is unsteady I've probably rolled it more times than I can remember. Luckily, it always pops back in place. There are only two thoughts racing through my head. "Don't touch the line before the whistle blows. Don't go before the whistle." My head is down and I close my eyes and visualize touching each line. The sweat pours down my face as I look up at the 5 lines ahead of me.

"One minute, if you all go full force the first time. If I see anyone slacking or not giving it your all, you will all do it again and again and again. You ARE only as good as your weakest link." I look up from the corner of my eye as the sweat continues to drip in my eyes. I look to my right where four people are barely hanging in there. I've already changed my clothes ten times today. I look at my feet and my shirt hangs heavy against the ground. I glance to my left. 6 people's heads are down and ready to run. The whistle blows. I'm running full speed. My hand touches down one line and I sprint back to the other and then sprint ahead towards the next and back again and again. I leap over the last line and grab the fence all while waiting for my breathing to calm. I soak my towel in cold water and hang it over my face as I lean back on the fence.

Here comes the next racing thought, "Qualifying for Nationals is just a few weeks away and the top college scouts will be in attendance. This is the moment you've trained for all these years." The whistle blows again. I drop my head and the towel falls to my hands. "Great job today guys. See you tomorrow. Get to bed early. You're done." In unison, we all say, "Thanks, coach." Not planned... just happened.

My dad is waiting for me at the gate. "How was it?" He smiled, put one hand on my shoulder, and hands me a Gatorade bottle in the other. "Brutal." He smiled again and we walk to the car. As soon as I feel the air conditioning hit my face, my eyes, I'm out. I feel the car slow down and make a left turn. I'm startled by the bumpy road beneath me and wake up to see that we're on a dirt road. "This isn't 7-11." My dad doesn't say anything as the car slows down. "Dad, I really want a Butterfinger dipped in a Coke Slurpee. That's what I want right now, and it's pretty clear that I need a shower." He stops the car and says, "Get out." He smiles. "You're not funny." He's still looking at me. "What do you want me to do?" He unlocks the door and says, "You're going to run the last mile home." I check to make sure that my seatbelt is locked in. It is. "What?! You have officially lost your mind. I'm exhausted. Dad, that road is all jacked up. Look at it. There are potholes everywhere. What if I roll my ankle before the tennis tournament? There goes my scholarship all those years of hard work out the door." "Get out." His voice is stern. I reluctantly get out and stand by the door and say to him, "Do you hear that?" I point towards the tall grassy field leading up to a large forest in the distance. "What are you talking about?" He says. "Yeah, the animal kingdom that's screaming at me right now. You can't hear the wild pheasants planning their aerial attacks? Let's not leave out the factor of the rabid squirrels that are planning ground assaults as well. They are 100% going after my Achilles tendons... both of them... I mean if you're good with a scene from the movie "The Birds" going down right now. They are hovering."

Now, he's really laughing. I got him. Yes, I don't have to do this, and then I hear it, "Jennifer." It's all in the tone. I shut the door and hear the click of the door lock and with a grin, he motioned me forward. So I start running. I keep looking back and he keeps motioning me forward. No headphones, just me and the uneven pavement. I hear the tires grinding against the dirt behind me and in complete rocky style our blue Sable, aka the blue dolphin, keeps a steady pace. I can't see my house but I visualize the road home all while I pivot over potholes and tune out the wild animal sounds coming from the distance. They were not going to steer me off course. I was focused on my goal. I saw it. I visualized the finish line the last step in my accomplishment, the smooth pavement ahead. I jump over the last cement step in front of my house just as my dad pulls into the drive way. He smiles and says, "Get in." I got my Butterfinger and dipped it in my Coke Slurpee and it was the jam!

Later in life, I look back at the last mile as a metaphor for my life. My dad knew I had it in me to finish the last mile even though I was exhausted and didn't think I had more to give, but he believed in me and knew I did. I just didn't believe in myself. There is always more mojo juice to squeeze out of you and I knew that I needed to push myself a little harder out of my comfort zone. That's when greatness happens.

My dad always says to me, "Life will be filled with potholes and uneven pavement but how you adapt and pivot will determine how you show up in the world."

I was tested at a young age when my parents went through a horrendous and contentious divorce. My dad received full custody of me when I was five years old. With him being an only child that was now raising a daughter on his own was an example of the strength that my dad possessed.

My dad has always been there, encouraging me since a young age, and most importantly being present as he learned to navigate this new chapter of our life. He quit his sales job to become a teacher to ensure he could be at my practices and tournaments. This was tennis practice— six days a week and traveling to tournaments on the weekends. I never once heard him complain about the hours of practices he went to, or his decision to switch his career or how it impacted his own personal life. Every time I won a trophy, or was written up in the newspaper, he was so proud. You could see the smile in his eyes and hear it in his voice. I wasn't just reeling in my glory of my own accomplishments but I was winning for us. That is the definition of true legacy in my eyes.

Just when I thought things were going as planned, it happened. I was gearing up to go to college, and I got a call that my mother had a heart attack and was on life support. There were so many emotions that I was dealing with from our strained relationship over the years. We didn't see eye to eye, and I held a grudge regarding how my mother treated my father during their marriage and post-divorce. I could never understand why she tried to compete with him over me. I wasn't a trophy. I was a child who loved both parents. I wasn't going to let anyone talk about my dad in such a way that I felt was disrespectful. He was the one showing up every single day and always had my back. I stopped talking to her because of it. My dad never said an ill word about her to me ever... not once. He has patience that I aspire to have to this day.

I still see the horrific scene play out in my head just like a movie. The gray clouds cover the heavy atmosphere. Not even a hint of a sunbeam can break through the clouds. My dad drives me to the hospital and the car isn't fully stopped yet and I jump out of the car. I keep thinking this is a joke right, not real, right? I blaze into the emergency room and I see my aunts and uncle were there lingering outside a door. They hold out their arms, "Oh, Jennifer." I blow past them and enter the room to see my grandma hysterically crying and howling over my mother who lays motionless on the bed. There were so many IV's pumping fluids into her body. She was so bloated that I thought for a moment that it couldn't be her but it was. It is an image that will forever be burned into my psyche. The doctor says, "She's brain dead. There's not much else we can do." It was the end. I rush out of the room trying to find a bathroom to lose my shit, not literally, but I needed my space.

Now, I'm processing all of the scenarios racing around in my head. I'm angry. I'm hurt because we didn't have a close relationship and there will be no chance of fixing that. I'm moving far away from my family, alone, scared, and floundering in a few months.

I vividly remember looking into the mirror saying you're fine, you can do this, you didn't come this far to give up now, pushing the sadness and anger deeper within me. I'm tough enough. I can do this one on my own. I couldn't have been more wrong. I told myself that I didn't need therapy. What I needed most in that moment was a mental coach. This is why it is so important to be coachable in life.

You need coaches and mentors in life. I was fortunate to have several coaches and mentors starting from a very young age. My dad was instrumental by being my first and best coach. When I was around 12-years-old, that's when my tennis level shifted and we needed specialists in different areas to heighten my strengths and work through the weakness of my game. I had a coach that specialized in groundstrokes; I had a serve and volley coach, strategy coach, and personal trainer. This was integral in my road to my dream. I couldn't be the best version of myself if I wasn't committed to listen and learn from those who were highly specialized in their area of expertise. That's why mentors are so important.

I have coaches to this day, because how can you grow and be the best version of yourself without looking at the reflection in the mirror and asking for help, and learn from others successes and failures. If you look at the most successful people in the world, they all have had mentors, coaches and advisory boards they lean on for advice.

You have to want to work hard. I had to push through even when I thought I was done but I had more to give. The hard work paid off. I received a tennis scholarship to play Division 1 tennis and I played number 1 for Coastal Carolina University. My dad was brilliant to put me in sports at a young age. I needed an outlet and tennis was a great way to learn team building, perseverance, and the trials of winning and losing. There were so many times that I wanted to quit and give up... so many times... but my dad never let me. He knew my potential even if I couldn't see it in that moment. I had issues with my wrists, ankles, and my shoulder. I was serving around 90 miles an hour at one point. If my mind and body aren't working in tandem how can I achieve my goal? I set my intention and goal at an early age and put it out into the universe.

My intentions and clear goals were crucial in opening doors that I never knew were even possible. I moved to Washington, DC after college, and was able to teach tennis at my aunt and uncle's country club. I was able to network with the members while looking for a job. I was the expert on the court and most of the members that I taught were CEOs. They provided sound advice which gave me an advantage when I went full-time into the workforce. I was able to use the strategies I learned from an early age and adapt those principles into successful businesses.

You have to love yourself. Everything starts with you. You can't focus on what you want out of life or be in a healthy sustaining relationship if you don't love yourself first. We are our own worst critics. I know, because I'm my own. There was a point in my life that I looked in the mirror and saw a ghost of the person I once was. I didn't stay in my lane, and I let the negativity of others veer me off my path just like the crazy pheasants in the wilderness tried during the last mile home.

I needed to get back to my 17-year-old self because she was a warrior. She showed up every day and was focused and I look back and wonder when I lost my spark. I let others dull my sparkle because they were petrified I would outshine them. The bullying and negativity of other people started to seep in slowly, and then become wildly rampant in my daily thoughts and belief system. I believed them when they harped at me, saying,

"You're not smart enough. You're just going to fail. Just another silly little hobby."

"You have a third-grade education."

"You're not pretty enough, what do you think you're some kind of model?"

"Look at you. You need to get back in the gym. You should probably get a trainer at least 5 times a week."

"You just sell phone systems that is not a real job, it's not like you are saving lives."

The irony of the last comment was the fact that this is exactly what I do. I find where vulnerabilities lie within companies' communication infrastructures and fix it. We are saving lives all around the world.

I will never forget a meeting I had with one of my non-profits years ago. We were packed into a small conference room waiting for my client to come in. They had volunteers putting together holiday donations to send to women and their families in need. I glanced over at the boxes that were waiting to be sealed and they were filled to the brim with clothes, diapers, wipes, toys, and games. I gaze back at my notes. My client rushed in and she is rattled. She has my full attention. She glances at me while putting her red glasses down on the table and her hands pull back and forth on the lower part of her neck, "Jen, we literally cannot have one call in our call center go unanswered. Not one. It is life or death."

That was a huge shift for me. Sometimes you can't see the impact of your work in the world and neither can others at that moment in time. This goes back to the visualization that I had to believe in while running the last mile. I couldn't see the smooth pavement ahead of me but I believed it was there. I just had to start running. These are the tools that my dad still reminds me of to this day. He is still my biggest supporter and coach. This is why you should never judge someone else's journey.

We need to be kind to one another because you never know what battle they may be going through especially on social media platforms. Social media is a great example of this. I say, "Never let a timeline feed get you twisted on your own personal journey." You never know what is really going on behind closed doors. We all wear masks every day. All of us. No one is immune to it because we are vulnerable beings and hide behind them. We need to strip away the layers of past experiences if we want to truly be seen.

It's all about patterns that we set that are intentional. If we can set a pattern of positive behavior first thing in the morning that shapes the day. We should all be waking up and looking at the reflection in the mirror and say, "I love you. You're enough. Let's rock this life. It's going to be an amazing day." It shapes your perspective. Period. It's practice. You need to train your brain. That's why you need an outlet and a tribe of positive people that want to rise you up not tear you down.

Find your tribe. They are your vibe. It's all about your tribe. My tribe fuels the blood and energy that courses through my veins. They are my lifeblood. Who you surround yourself with directly influences your path in life. If you surround yourself with negativity, negativity will come. If you surround yourself with positivity, positivity will come. I'm a firm believer that everyone that crosses your path in your own life journey is meant to teach you a lesson. Those lessons can be tough, cruel and even painfully brutal. But it's a test to see if you can re-engineer the circumstance into a positive one. We are tested every day.

There were times not only in tennis, but when I was being bullied, that I wanted to curl up in a ball and not leave my house. My dad would be there encouraging me and say, "This day too shall pass." He was right but there was also that voice inside my head that saying, "Negative Ghost Rider. Not today." If you don't fight for truth, justice, and accountability, the bullies win." I wasn't about to let that happen. When I shifted my mindset and not let fear run amuck, my perspective changed. I wasn't going to live like that anymore. When I found myself in the position of being bullied I trained my brain to ignore them. It was hard. I literally don't see them. They are ghosts to me even if they are standing right in front of me. I imagine holding a mirror in front of me and the venomous words just reflect off the glass. I will not let those words affect me because it is merely a reflection of how unhappy they are with themselves. My dad reminds me to always be mindful how you react in a situation.

No regrets. Regret is probably one of my biggest fears. It is the kryptonite of my soul. I don't want to have to look back and say... I wish I would have... if I just would have tried harder or asked for help when I needed, but I didn't have the courage and I didn't believe in myself enough. No, I can't let fear live in my space it doesn't belong there. This applies to personal relation-ships and the dating world as well. What if you pushed yourself out of your comfort zone when you had the chance? What could your life have been like? What if you put your phone down at Starbucks and made eye contact with people? Don't let life pass you by because you're not aware of life moving around you. You could miss a pivotal opportunity. If you see that attractive girl or guy walking down the street, say hi. Don't be scared. You never know. It's literally two letters. Don't let fear seep in.

I will never forget one day I was getting my hair done and my stylist's young assistant was helping me but she wasn't acting like her normally bubbly self. I asked her what was wrong and she told me that her and her boyfriend had broken up. She started tearing up and her eyes were already puffy. She was devastated. I said, "What happened?" I watched her face when she pulled the black smock over me. Her hands were shaking as she buttoned it around my neck. She told me that they got into a silly fight and that she was just being stubborn. You could hear the regret in her voice when she said he was the love of her life. She said, "I can't imagine my life without him." I took a deep breath in and said, "Have you told him how you really feel?" She shook her head no and started crying. It reminded me of a time when I wish someone was sitting in that very chair I was sitting in, and telling me to take a chance and speak my truth but I was too scared to run the last mile and the opportunity slipped right through my fingertips.

Life has a very funny and clever way of being cyclical. So, I told her my story. I looked up at her and said, I've been right where you are. I've been in the very shoes you're standing in. I was completely and ecstatically in love with someone and he too was the love of my life in my eyes." I tried to fight back the tears but some made their way down the smock. I said, "I didn't have the courage to say that I was in love with him and my true feelings and intentions. I wasn't strong enough. I was scared of what his response might be or having my heart broken." She was tuned into every word.

I sat in the steel chair and I could feel the tightness in my chest as the regret started to make its home in my heart again and I held it in. I take another deep breath in and say, "I still to this day see exactly where I was during that phone conversation. He asked me questions that I didn't want to answer. He literally asked me how I felt about him and I choked on my own silence. It felt like someone had stolen my voice. He asked me again how I felt and I deflected and next thing I knew the call was over. That moment and opportunity slipped away faster than I could have imagined because I wasn't honest with myself and with him. He was forever gone and he moved on. It was over.

Now, I have to live with that every day for the rest of my life because I didn't speak my truth. That's why the regret train is not the one I want to be on." She nodded. I said, "But, what if I told him how I really felt, would that made a difference? Maybe... Maybe not, but the fact is that I hid behind fear and "the cool girl" bravado. The only purpose that it served to me was the direct destination to loneliness, regret, and solitude." She thanked me for the talk, but I wanted to thank her for letting me talk my truth. Probably the best crescendo of the story is, now many years later, they are getting married. Who knows if my story shined a light on her or not but I felt it needed to be shared. Probably more for me as I navigate my own journey.

Most of us are in control of our own destiny and the way we are allowed to be who we really want to be is to be coachable, build the right tribe around you, don't live in regret and run the hell out of that last mile. Now, it's your chance to shift your destiny. What is the thing you are going to do, that you are going to push yourself just as far as you really need to go instead of sitting in a space of regret and worried that you will never be who you really want to be?

When you can feel in your core
you were destined for more
Keep that flame alive
Never let it burn out
We all have a purpose
And it's for the greater good
Personal sacrifice is a given
Never give up
Someone you don't know yet is counting on you
That person is your future self
You just have to run the last mile

Jen Hecht has an extensive background in both sales and marketing. Her innovative way of thinking allows her to connect the business principles she has learned over the years to the dating world. Jen is deeply committed to, and passionate about, helping others build a strong support system in their lives.

Nikki-Monique Kurnath

Mirrors, Mirrors... On The Walls Of Life

"You do not attract what you want.
You attract what you are."
~Wayne Dyer

When was the last time you found yourself standing in front of a mirror, really looking at the person right before you? Was it today? Or was it yesterday? Or maybe it was over a week ago. As you stop for a moment and think about it... do you remember what you saw? How did you feel when you saw your own reflection? Were you, Happy? or Proud? Or did you feel Sadness? or Disappointment? Did you ever ask yourself... 'WHO AM I?!'

I'll admit it, I've done this before... actually many times before. Especially throughout my teenage years and up until recently, when I realized enough was enough. How many times did I need to keep sabotaging myself with those 'warped mirrors' that were found in my life? Why did I need to go through challenge after challenge, in order to find out WHO and WHAT I really am made of? Did I need to continue punishing myself with the pressures that I was just NOT good enough? Not smart enough... not beautiful enough... not talented enough and definitely not rich enough? Whatever happened to the self-love and gratitude that I was supposed to have and feel about myself? Where was it hiding behind those so-called mirrors in my life?

I know life is filled with its ups and downs, and it's not perfect. That's why it's called the 'roller coaster of life'. But it's up to YOU and how you 'handle the ride' with the situations that you are faced with. Along with the people that are 'guests' riding along with you, you change and evolve depending on what highs and lows you experience… individually and collectively. God knows I've tried to remain positive when I was blindsided with negativity in the past, but let's be honest here… it's not freakin easy! Especially if you don't have the proper support system around you, to guide you through it and bring you back to safety after you feel like you've crashed. Those dark times, through the tunnels of life, can seem like they go on forever. You may end up losing a part of yourself that you may sadly, never ever get back.

Not to sound cliché, but I wasn't popular in high school. I had some girls that were my friends, but none of us were part of the 'in' crowd. I didn't participate in any sport teams or academic clubs really. The only thing I can genuinely remember is that I really enjoyed attending my Drama class. The teacher was fun and entertaining and I liked the idea that you could transform yourself and become anyone that you wanted to be. Even though I auditioned for many of the principal roles in the school plays, I sadly didn't get them. They would often go to the most popular students in the school, which was no surprise. Funny how those drama classes and the roles within them; along with the chorus roles that I did end up being cast for, helped me to learn how to hide my 'true self' from the world, when I was faced looking into the cracked mirrors of my life. Who knew that my ordinary role of a good student and a behaved daughter was going to end up looking more like a soap opera slut instead?

Being the oldest child and the first daughter to my European parents meant that I was initially the one to do many things first and on my own. My mother was now working in a job after staying home for 14 years to take care of my siblings and I. We were lucky in a way, because we didn't experience daycare or even babysitters that much while growing up. We seemed to be a close-knit family back then when we were all much younger. My father was the only bread winner for the first 14-years, which meant that money was tight at times, having to support a family of five. While I was growing up, I remember my parents supporting me and my interests as they paid for my music, skating and dancing lessons and my extracurricular activity too as a Girl Guide/Pathfinder. As I loved horses, I would also ask if I could have a horse of my own, however my parents had to remind me there was no space for one at our house. As the costs of my activities increased as I became better at developing those skills and started to advance to higher responsibilities, my parents did what they could until they had to stop. They also had to take care of my other two siblings and their extra-curricular activities as well, therefore I couldn't be selfish. Since I was told that there was no future in those kinds of fields, and that these were just hobbies, I was no longer supported to continue with them throughout my high school years. Did I blame my parents at that time? Definitely yes! I was a discouraged and hurt teenager. The more I loved those activities, the more the sacrifices hurt. They made me feel so good about myself. How I felt when I would look into the mirror, as the Skater, the Dancer and the Musician. It helped me to express myself artistically and creatively. Only later in life would I recognize how my parents did their best to provide love, guidance and discipline towards their children, once I too became a parent myself. I wish I knew I needed to forgive them even though at times it was hard, especially bearing in mind their strict rules or harsh punishments while growing up over the years. At that age, I wanted to resent them. I wanted them to be there for me… in many different ways. I know now as an adult, my parents did what they could to accommodate me at that time, with the knowledge and resources that they had available to them. Whatever they couldn't do or provide to me, was because they didn't know how to do it first for themselves.

There was obvious pressure to do my best in high school too. It amplified with time. I didn't want to disappoint my parents after all, but I felt like I always did somehow. Without knowing my place or purpose, I questioned my competence and compared myself to others during my teenage years, even within my own family. It felt like the award for the smartest child seemed to go to my sister because of her higher grades while my brother stood out as the funniest child with his great sense of humor. I was ordinary and felt uncomfortable in my own skin, as I began looking into the teenage mirrors of my life and not loving what I was seeing. Even though I was called 'Unique Monique', I felt that unique was different... but in a bad way. I knew I wanted improvements in my life but I didn't know how to get them. What did I need to do in order to stand out as something special and be unique after all?

Be careful what you wish for, because you might get it. Once you get it, be careful as you just might not know what to do with it.
~Unknown

The girls I would hang out with in high school had their stumbling blocks as well. They would have fights with their parents or siblings too, and although their school marks were good, they weren't excellent either. They were considered pretty, but they were not popular girls by any means either. It's true what they say that, "Birds of a feather flock together." We seemed to be there for one other, however not in the way that I really wished they had. Once I started to change in a dangerous way, they too started changing for the worse. The mirrors in my life became more so like the crazy mirrors at a fun house. It felt like a circus, just without all the fun.

The pressure to date in high school and lose your virginity, as a girl, was pretty intense. Though I really wasn't interested in having a boyfriend at that age, the peer pressure from a couple of my girlfriends towards my later high school years, were pretty prevalent. I didn't know how I could keep brushing off the subject and avoid talking about having sex, since I really wanted to wait until I was married and fall deeply in love.

As we lived in a small town, our typical high school parties were either house parties when the parents weren't around, or field parties in the country streets outdoors. All these get-togethers would mainly include some form of kegs of beer and available "weed" – marijuana. As I was always afraid of the punishments if I were to get caught by my parents for doing something illegal or wrong, I would try my sample of a toke or a sip or two of beer at one of these events with my girlfriends but rarely got carried away. That's of course until I lost who I was in my mirror of self-loathing and became someone else that I no longer was connected or recognized to.

When I met him, he was a senior, finishing his last year in our high school. I was a junior, about to turn 17 that year. I didn't know anything about him as I wasn't in the popular crowd which he hung out with. A couple of my girlfriends knew who he was, as they shared their mutual thoughts of how they were crushing on him, when they would see him in school. When he approached me at one of these parties and said "Hi", I actually thought he was saying it to someone else. When he said it again and introduced himself, I realized that he was actually speaking to me. That's when I also realized how gorgeous he was standing in front of me, being so close. I was taken aback. Surprisingly when I was about to introduce myself, he interrupted me and said my name first, as if he had memorized it to impress me. Funny enough, I was impressed! We talked that night for a bit but when I didn't accept his offer for beer and a joint, he then said 'Bye' and left. I was a bit disappointed but it was one of my girlfriends actually, that took it much harder. She told me I screwed up and not to be such a 'goody-goody' or a 'nun' and instead party more with alcohol and drugs like the rest of the popular kids were doing. I knew better, but now Mr. Popular had planted a seed in my mind. I was finding it much harder to stay true to who I wanted to be.

The next time I saw this popular guy in school, I finally noticed him walking past me, at the other end of the hall from my locker. His eyes met mine and a big smile began to form on his smooth shaved face. He started to walk towards me, as I quickly turned my head, pretending to look for something in my locker. As I was feeling nervous yet excited in my stomach suddenly, I realized that he was right beside me! He began to make small talk and then he had asked me out for our first date. I couldn't believe it... ME! He chose me! When I told my girlfriends, they were so excited and happy for me. They helped me plan what to wear and when it was time to meet him, they told me how 'lucky' I was, going on a date with a guy like this. Little did I know, how this one date would forever, change my life.

He picked me up at my house that night after my parents had left for the cottage that weekend. We went out for dinner, he brought me home, and then he asked where my parents were. I told him they were away with my siblings at the cottage up north. He asked if he could come in for a bit to watch TV together. Oblivious at the time, I thought this is what you should do during this part of your date. Even though I had a family room on the main floor of my house with a comfy couch and a TV in it, my date wanted to take a tour around the floor and asked what was in the basement. I explained that it was the rec room and he began to go downstairs. Though it's been years since my family and I have lived in that house, I can still remember now where the TV was situated, sitting on the carpeted floor and how the old couch was there too, which was a sofa bed, all closed up.

I recall Mr. Popular asking for some alcohol to drink since my dad's bar was in the basement too, but I reminded him that my parents didn't know I was out with him and that he wasn't allowed to drink any of my dad's booze. Disappointment seemed to appear on his face as he rolled his eyes up and around, and I remembered my girlfriend's words in my mind 'Have more fun!', especially with a guy like this.

My parents had a cold storage in that basement and what I remembered doing next was one of my biggest mistakes. I opened the door, looking for some old bottles of homemade currant wine that I remembered my parents had made from our other family home which was stored away in that cold storage. I found a few homemade bottles hidden in a corner and grabbed one out. Labeled with the year and not much else, it was a shade of reddish pink and I knew that it was an aged wine. My date grabbed it quickly out of my hands and went to my dad's bar to grab a couple of glasses. Next thing I knew, the bottle was open, and suddenly the drinks began to pour... lots of it, even though I wasn't sure if I was really ready for any of this. The flavor had a strong, sour taste to it. The TV was now somehow on, but I didn't have a chance to even focus on it.

I do recall that my date wanted to dance with me and suddenly there was music playing from the stereo. At this point, I know I was getting tipsy but I remember still trying to stay in control, even though Mr. Popular kept refilling my glass after my sip or two. Was he trying to get me drunk or something as he kept saying "You're drinking too slow. Keep up!"? He continued to bring the glass to my mouth, pushing me to drink more. By then I was not feeling good and wanting to slow down, but he wasn't listening to me. He would pick me up from the couch and squeezed me tight, as we drunkenly swayed back and forth to whatever music that was playing. I don't even think it was a slow song. I was feeling dizzy and confused. I wasn't having fun anymore. I asked him to stop and let's sit down and talk for a bit.

I don't know how it happened still to this day, but I suddenly was falling onto the couch... or was I thrown to the couch by him? Accidently banging my head didn't help. Maybe that was why the whole room was spinning now. My stomach was churning. I felt I was going to be sick! I was forgetting where I was, as it was dark in my basement with only the light coming from the TV, as the sound was muted or the music was louder to cover up the TV sounds. The whole situation was unclear, and it didn't matter to me. All I wanted to do was have him leave my house now. All I wanted to do was go to sleep in my bed and feel better in the morning. All I wanted to happen was to end this terrible night as I felt it was out of control. But sadly, my wishes didn't come true. Instead, just when I thought things couldn't get worse, they did.

What haunted me for years afterwards was the in and out moments of that shocking and dreadful night. How my arms and legs felt like dead weights as I couldn't move them around. How my whole body felt like it was in awful pain with a monstrous heaviness upon me-on my chest and stomach, then pressure on my back and especially in between my legs. How my face and neck ached and was sensitive to touch, and it was hard for me to breathe at times.

I remember fragments of a song playing in the background with the words '... I want your sex. I want your sex...' as I was feeling like I was awake in a nightmare. Many years later did I realize, that each time I heard that George Michael song, I would feel numbness throughout my entire being, as if it was protecting me from this unspeakable moment in time. I know I was saying 'Stop it! Stop it! Get off of me!' when this was happening to me, but nothing changed... nothing stopped. I was trapped. I was a prisoner in my own house and there was nothing... nothing I could do about it.

When I finally awoke, I heard nothing. There was silence. No music was playing. No TV was on. I was slowly adjusting my eyes to the darkness, except for the small morning light shining through the basement window. Then I felt it. I was lying naked... completely naked, laying on my stomach, on top of my sofa bed in the basement. The sofa bed was pulled out completely. I slowly turned around, as the wave of excruciating pain shocked my body... my head hurting, my arms aching and the scent of blood around me. There were lots of red blood spots all over the white bed sheet. I realized at this exact moment what really happened. He raped me! I was raped... raped by my date-Mr. Popular as I refer to him, in order to not say his real name out loud anymore. This asshole took advantage of me! I was passed out drunk like never ever before. He took away my innocence during my 17th year of life. He took away my virginity in a horrific way, without my consent. I was feeling so lost, scared, confused, angry, and ashamed. How could someone that I liked or who I thought liked me, do something so unimaginable like THIS to me?! I didn't know what to do. The only thing I could think of was to curl up and just die. How could something like this have happened to me? What did I do so wrong that I deserved something so bad like this to occur?

I knew I needed to talk to someone about this, but who? My parents wouldn't understand. They would be mad at me for stealing the homemade wine, drinking it, having a boy over at our house and not telling them... the list went on. I decided to call my girlfriend who lived on the north hill and told her I needed to see her. Though I didn't have a car to drive yet at that time, I didn't care. I just had to get out of that basement, that house and get out. I threw on some pieces of clothing over my aching body as I then saw my reflection, standing in the mirror. I saw the marks that I was covering up, marks that he left on my body as he violated me. I hated myself for letting this guy do this to me. I started blaming myself more and more. I was so disgusted with the girl that I saw standing before me.

As I walked like a zombie to my girlfriend's house, I don't remember how long it took to get there. It was as if time stood still. Sadly, my girlfriend wasn't the best help as she expressed she was 'happy' that I finally did it and could join 'the club' with the other girls, She didn't get it. She couldn't understand what really happened here. The sad part is no one did. There were two other incidents after that before anyone realized what Mr. Popular was doing to me. He was blackmailing me, telling me to stay with him, that I was drunk, I was a slut and I was just having second thoughts. Yet I knew this was NOT me. I knew I DIDN'T want this. I didn't want to have sex like this with him. It was against my will. I never knew when it was going to happen next so I made sure to never be with him alone again.

But he always found a way to get to me. The worse was when I stopped it from ever happening again. He then fulfilled his threat and began spreading rumors about me in high school that I was a 'Drunk Slut.' I was feeling so alone and misunderstood. My life felt like a bad soap opera. I felt like I was being killed off. The mirrors in my life were all shattered to pieces along with my self-esteem, loss of love and respect for who I was, and from the damage of what others closest to me thought of me.

A full-year later, once we were ready to graduate, I recall that girlfriend of mine confronted me, and said she was sorry she wasn't there for me when I really needed it. She witnessed the terrible name calling and how it destroyed who I was during that senior year. My girlfriend was scared and didn't know what to do at that time. None of us did. My parents didn't understand what was happening to me as our relationship became more strained. We went to counseling trying to figure things out, but I couldn't talk about what happened to me with anyone else.

I was the victim and I kept having that mentality throughout my life, as I continued to attract more negativity into it. But one day I realized 'Enough was enough!' Once I discovered how to change my mindset from Victim to Survivor, I started to become whole once again. Though I was broken and scarred, I was not going to allow that to kill me. I began to go deeper into myself and learn to let go of the Post-Traumatic Stress (PTS) that I was storing in my subconscious mind. I started expanding my world, started connecting myself closer to God and learning about the powers of the Universe. I started discovering what healthy self-care techniques were all about, and learning more about Affirmations. I also discovered how important it was to rebuild my relationship with the 'Mirrors in my Life'.

As an adult, I started bringing "Mirror Maintenance," daily into my life, as I set a goal for myself to improve my mindset for 28 days without the use of medications. I did not want to start with prescription pills that were going to control my thoughts. I wanted to be IN CONTROL of who I am born to be. Tuning out the negative noise of others and their opinions about me, was another one of my goals. I needed to draw out the positive self-love that I desired within me. I knew I was going to make it through, day by day, as I started to also learn about gratitude and journaling. I began to give permission for myself to heal and move forward and get back on that roller coaster called Life. No depression or anxiety was going to destroy me anymore. I knew that I was going to love again one day, more so, once I started to fall in love with myself first.

I decided to bury away that terrible loss of innocence as the young adult Monique died. I moved on to college, post-grad and then furthered my jobs/careers as I discovered two-sides of me in this world. One mirror reflected the outgoing Entertainer who was modeling, bartending, go-go dancing, touring etc. as I became Nikki. The other was the Social Advocate, like the Law Abiding Citizen as I was studying to be a police officer, then an immigration officer and then an entrepreneur as I started to grow a healthier Monique. After all these years of searching, I am proud to say, I know now "Who I Am..." a little bit of both. I have now found my balance in my life, as I started just last year. I know who I am and I am grounded with a stronger sense of my identity with love, respect, truth and forgiveness.

Loneliness is the poverty of self. Solitude is the richness of self.
~ May Sarton

Practicing SELF-LOVE and bringing it back into my life was one of the healthiest decisions I ever made! Being THANKFUL daily, for what I have, and not focusing on what I don't have, also made a huge difference in my life. Learning how the Law of Attraction works and having faith in God to help me along the way, really all brought it together. I was starting to change and transform from that blankly staring Monique, to becoming that Unique Monique, and now Nikki-Monique. I am thankful to the discovering of falling in love with myself once again as I am healing from the past and am mindful of my present. I am becoming confident with my own reflection in the "mirrors on the walls" of my life. I AM smarter, sweeter, sexier and stronger, as each day I just keep getting better and better in my life and continue to love and be loved, with who I am born to be.

Attract what you Expect. Reflect what you Desire.
Become what you Respect. Mirror what you Admire.
~Dalai Lama

Monique Kurnath C.Ht., CCYT (aka Nikki-Monique) is a Well-Fit Specialist, Certified Hypnotherapist, Speaker/Host, Reiki Practitioner, Spokesmodel and Certified Children's Yoga Teacher. She's passionate about helping women & children #BMPOWHERD through wellness and fitness from a Holistic Health prospective. She's a dedicated single mama of a talented loving son.

April Nicolas

You are Stronger than You Think:

Obstacles are Detours in the Right Direction

Did you ever think you would end up here, yes, you in your present life today? If you are like me, with all the winding roads that it took to get here, I forgot about the destination that I had in mind. I do remember the feeling that I wanted to feel. Stick with me because it does get better.

I am 44 years old today, I have a beautiful 15-month old baby girl named Luna who I had on my 43rd birthday, married to my best friend, my perfect mirror, the one who helps me to heal, stretch, grow and remember the truth of who I really am. I also have a 17½ year old young lady going on 30, Ariana and a Zen, 14½ year old boy who is most likely my greatest teacher, Mateo. We have 3 dogs, 1 cat and lots of love in our home. It is perfect in all its imperfections; for a blended family we are full of our share of the usual teenager mood swings and boundary testing. I am reminded that— if that didn't happen, we weren't parenting right. I also have to say, that when something is not right with our teenagers, they will crawl in bed with us and cry as we hold them close, kiss them, and let them know that it's all going to be okay. We have a foundation that is solid, we have hiccups, but we know that we stick like glue when things go wrong. All is well in our world. We are solid where it counts. It wasn't always this way, because if you knew me you would know...

I am the oldest of 5, raised to be the perfect example child, nothing I did was ever good enough, my father was an alcoholic/drug addict, mother was a "rager" and someone who had to tell white lies to survive. I grew up seeing my mom emotionally, mentally, physically abused. We ran away from my dad and our country of origin and went on the run at the age of 10. In 1984, we came to the United States with 2 suitcases, 5 kids and a broken mother. We then moved in with her parents where a history of incest was a secret. To give you an idea— my brother was killed through gang violence at 17, my middle sister was molested by my mom's father, then she looked for love in all the wrong places and was pregnant at 13 and a drug addict at 15, my youngest sister had issues with men/trust and my youngest brother was in and out of "Juvi" by the age of 12. I was my mom's partner, mother, father and I was the parent to my siblings. There was no love left for me. I then spent all my energy trying not to marry somebody like my dad. That, however, was exactly what I manifested. I am the niece, the daughter, the sibling, an ex fiancé, an ex wife, of an alcoholic/drug addict. This is my story in a nutshell.

It is so weird how I can retrieve more negative memories than I can of having fun and loving life. At the age of 3, I ran away because my mom brought home our middle sister and told me that we had to share everything with her. I was not a very happy big sister. I took my little brother and we went over to our neighbor's backyard where we can see over our yard. After what seemed like forever, nobody called to have us come home or look for us. We were forced to go home to eat by our stomachs and say hello to our crying sister at home.

At the age of 4, I ran to the bathroom while my dad and mom were fighting, he was hitting her again and I figured I would stay in the bathroom till they were done. I sat there in fear until I thought I heard words telling me that it was all a part of a test and that it would make sense one day. I don't know whose voice it was, or why it brought me such peace, but I trusted it. I was later to realize that it wasn't a voice that I heard but more of a knowing from within.

When I was 8 my dad was in Taiwan working a gig. He spent all his earnings on alcohol, drugs and women, so we were kicked out of our home and our belongings thrown onto the street. I watched as strangers dragged our belongings from a 3-story house onto the sidewalk. My mom hanging on a man's leg as he was carrying a piece of furniture out, begging him not to do this, and to give her more time. I was carrying my 2 youngest siblings, as I watched everything as it happened, I vowed right there and then that this would never happen again to our family. At this point, there wasn't much that I cried about as a kid, I learned to roll with the punches and to get tough, to meet what was ahead.

By the time I was 18, I learned that there were certain norms; how to juggle things, how to fix, how to put out fires for everybody around me. I held our family together the best I could but saving people who didn't want to help themselves became exhausting and left me depleted.

I was 19-years-old when my brother passed away. I was angry at God, I questioned all the religion they tried to shove down my throat. At his funeral, the minister told me that I would be a healer one day. I didn't know why he said that to me, he didn't even know who I was. The year after my brother's passing was a blur. I can't remember a single event except that I smoked a lot of cigarettes and I had a lot of sleepless nights. My sister was heavy in her drug use, we didn't know if the next phone call was going to be about her getting arrested again, or if she had overdosed or something worse. We all helped out in raising my niece to the best of our abilities given we had school and I also had a job. At this point, my mom had lost all hope, she was deep in her depression and I can only imagine. No parent should have to bury their child, it is unthinkable.

Remember in the beginning I said I spent so much energy trying not to be with somebody like my dad that, was exactly what I manifested. Everything is energy at its core. I dated the same type of guys who had a big heart and the potential to be the one. I was told later, that these are the effects of addiction in families. We either became addicts or we became people affected by it, with our own issues. My future wasn't painted very brightly, but nobody told me not to try so, I went after my goals. I worked at a young age, supported my family financially, and in all other ways. I paid my own way to get braces, to get through college while working at the same time and had amazing relationships with people. If people saw me or spoke with me they never knew the story behind the face.

Time went on, and I married my high school sweetheart after being reunited with him 9-years after we met and soon after my break up with my ex fiancé who was also an addict. The flags were all there, in bright neon colors letting me know of the commonalities, the similarities of character in the men that I chose to date, key word here, chose. Don't get me wrong, I also dated men without an addiction, in fact one of them had a doctorate degree from MIT in Nuclear Engineering. My mother had told me to marry this one, and, I still laugh at that to this day. He was great, one of the most wonderful experiences of my life, without drama. There was just something there that was missing. I sensed at 20-years-old, that I would be bored. That is when people later say, "that people like us, our pickers are broken because we attract the same kind of people into our lives that brought us problems," in this case my alcoholic father. My friends use to simply say that I was attracted to bad boys. It wasn't until recent years that I understood. I am not attracted to bad boys, but I wanted a good man that had naughty parts. Somebody who took chances in life is open to adventures and would risk it all for love.

Now, back to love; my first marriage to my High School sweetheart ended short of 12 years. I was engaged previously to somebody I dated for 6 years. Nobody ever gets married and says, I think I am done around 12 years. We all hope that it would last forever. I built the ideal life, the house with the white picket fence, the cars, the business, the 2 kids, the 2 dogs and all the bells and whistles that came with it. In that marriage I also learned how to redefine love unconditionally, how to forgive without resentment, how to be compassionate for somebody who I saw had no control over their life. I became an ugly person only because I never learned how to love and care for myself, as much as I was trained to care for everybody else. It took a very long time before I found peace in my life, but looking back, I can assure you that all the dots connect. Stay with me.

In the midst of my marriage with 2 young kids, I woke up one day and realized I was re-living my mom's life. I was married to a man who used alcohol and drugs, lied, cheated and stole from me. I slowly became numb without knowing it. My time and energy was best spent taking care of my 2 beautiful children, working full-time, running a business I helped build and making sure everything was running. I hid the ugly parts from my kids, so I thought. At the age of 34, my husband at the time, needed a pacemaker and I was a senior manager for a very large company. In 2007, I was 33 and I had to ask myself, what was life about? I quit my corporate job to spend time with the family.

It was during this time, that my world expanded to all the possibilities in life with all the coaching, studying, training, business and personal development that I was so hungry for. I needed to know why I was alive and what was I meant to do? I met a young man at work, full of life, hungry for adventure who had dreams for tomorrow, somehow, this reminded me of who I use to be before I became numb.

I can remember the day I told him that our journey as husband and wife was over. I came home thinking our mutual friend had told him, I saw his truck in the driveway, but as I searched the house, I panicked. I couldn't hear or see him anywhere in sight. Until I went back downstairs, and there he was in broad daylight napping on the couch, I knew right there and then that my love for him was based on the fact that I was in fear that without me, he wouldn't be okay. That wasn't the kind of love I wanted.

I woke him up and gave him the news. His reply was…"why, I haven't done anything lately." I smiled, I said "this is not about you, but me." I told him that I can feel Spirit, the Universe is urging me for something greater. I told him that we had to take a leap of faith and that this was going to change all our lives for the better. I continued to explain, "one day you will realize that I spared you." I reminded him that I spent my time and energy making sure that our family, our relatives, our friends were okay that I forgot all about me. Then it hit me, I was just as important as him, and everybody else, no more, no less. He didn't fully understand, but he accepted it, at first.

He wouldn't move out of our house to give me space, which I knew I needed to get some clarity in the situation. I needed to get things in order, we were just surviving financially at this point, he was spending as much as we were making in the business. I believe that I was given no choice, but to move out leaving everything behind, just taking my kids and starting new just like my mom did. Only this was moving 2 cities over and with the support of a lot of loving people that gave me strength because they had been there too. My ex promised to drag the divorce out for a long time, to make my life a living hell. I told him he can do whatever he wants, but that nothing can harm me because I was protected by Spirit, God, and the Universe. He rented out our house, that we had purchased with 200,000 cash down, a 3,500 square foot 2-story house with a pool that my kids grew up in. We moved to a 2-room duplex by my work, a place I made sure I can afford if he never gave me any financial support. My friends didn't understand, how I could feel happy in the midst of a divorce, losing my home, the comfort of 2 incomes, my marriage. I simply replied that I choose to be happy. I was happy before I got married, happy while married and determined to be happy after my divorce.

I borrowed against my 401K to hire a lawyer and to stay afloat just incase something else came up in the midst of the divorce process. In the meantime, I could sense that I was starting to feel alive again. Although, feeling grief towards my marriage, I began to feel like a woman again, not just somebody's wife and a mother of 2. I felt possibilities of the future. I have never given up on the idea that there was that one person for us. Most of all I felt my connection to my Higher Power getting stronger as I learned to trust in my own inner guidance. I began to lean toward that guidance with blind faith more and more. YES, I expected miracles. Guess what, they kept coming.

In 2012, I felt like the pieces of my life were finally falling into place. I wanted to start focusing on clearing space in my life to invite more love in. I decided to write a list of all the qualities I wanted in my future partner. I had 50 items on that list. At the same time, I decided to start loving myself more and got to know what made my heart smile. I practiced Bikram yoga, went for walks, exercising again, eating right and being mindful of my thoughts, words and actions. After writing that letter to my future partner, I was aware of signs that he was near. I also felt a spirit of a baby near me, but told it to come back after they have found their father. In 2013, I started to journal even more about my journey inside, studying under some amazing teachers, which continued from my studies in the past. My way of healing old wounds and understanding who I am and why I made the choices I made in the past.

I met my current husband in July 2013. There was a soul recognition, but the first thought I had was "don't touch that one." Little did I know, he said the same thing to himself, that he wasn't ready to get involved; we were both still trying to heal and understand ourselves from our previous relationships. A year after we met, I had asked him for a ride to a diner to wait for my niece who had my car. That was the beginning of everything we have today; everything I mentioned to you at the beginning of my story; our family, the spirituality that we practice with our connection and belief in something bigger than ourselves. The energy that runs through each and every-one of us, the essence that makes us unique but united.

In the early parts of my adulthood I did everything that came natural for me that I thought my purpose was something harder and different. I thought I had to be somebody other than myself, so I changed my major to be in business instead of following my heart and write. As a kid, I always pretended to be a teacher and writing on chalkboard with students or I was a boss that owned her own business. As I got older, I sorted within me what Divine Guidance is, taking away the guilt and shame that came with the religion I was raised with, and left with a connection to something bigger than anything but part of everything. That something that had watched over me as a child and assured me that everything was going to okay and that it was all going to make sense one day. As I mentioned, the minister at my brother's funeral that I would be a healer one day, however, I had forgotten about this until 20 years later while listening about our defining moment.

A defining moment is when something horrible is happening but something amazing is happening or being planted at the same time. When it is happening in the midst of the storm, we can't see, nothing makes sense, our world seems upside down. Nobody told me that our world sometimes had to be turned upside down to get right side up. You see, my brother Bong almost died at birth, he had to have a full blood transfusion to survive. He lived to be 17-years-old, to be my best friend, my partner in crime, my sidekick, my gift, my connection to the whole. One of my greatest defining moments is the day my brother died, but the gift is that somebody I didn't know gave me a message that stayed with me, a seed was planted; that I would be a healer one day. As I listened to the audio, a vision came to me, the string of events connecting everything leading to this current day. My brother played a role in my life, he had died so that I can feel that deep pain, sorrow and grief to be able to relate to all the people that I would be helping. How can I touch peoples' heart if I can't relate to them? How can I possibly tell them and show them that there is hope even when all hope seems lost, that the light at the end of the tunnel does exist even when everything around us seems dark and grim. I know this to be true because the day that I was listening to the audio was the same exact date that my brother had died 20 years earlier. I cried tears of joy and understanding because for the first time, I felt understanding for my sense of such deep loss. I knew what a miracle the unfolding of my life had been with all the twist and turns. What an amazing life we lead. Everything that doesn't make sense, as painful as they may be, sometimes there is a reason to why it is happening. A greater, bigger picture for the greater good of everybody involved.

Here on these pages are the chapters of my life that connected my life stories to who I am today. The mess that was my life became the message I would share with everybody who needed to hear it, to heal and understand their own path.

I know today, that everything in my life is connected and has a purpose as there are no accidents. I know that everybody is doing their best with what they have at all times. I know that all the hurdles and trials in our lives are just detours to the right direction. How do I know that? Looking back, it was all there in front of me right from the start; my DNA wired me to be a daughter of an addict, therefore I was drawn to addicts. If my parents weren't who they were, we, their kids wouldn't have been born. If my father wasn't who he was, my mom would have never left him to immigrate to the United States. I would have never met my ex-husband, I wouldn't have had my 2 wonderful kids, the greatest treasure from that marriage. If I wasn't a person affected by alcoholism, I would have never met my now husband, lover, best friend and father to all 3 of my kids. If I hadn't lost my brother, I wouldn't have gone down the path of spirituality to get some understanding on who I am, to get the healing and clarity. I needed to follow my own Spiritual guidance. Life was meant to be simple, never easy, but always relative to our own perception. I choose to see the lesson in the trials that life presents me, I choose to take 100% responsibility for how my life unfolds. I will continue to choose to believe in love instead of fear.

Every day I am faced with a choice in what comes first in my life. I have to remember to stay true to my heart and to do what feels good and right for me— to love and care for myself as I would my husband and children. The order in which it works for me is, I have to take care of myself, mind, body and soul along with my connection to my Higher Power, then it is my family, and all else follows. When stress comes to my life and I am freaking out, I remember to follow my breath and to keep things simple and to go back to basics; self-care. Worry is a waste of time. I am reminded that feeling overwhelmed is just a word. In reality, it is simply telling me that I feel unprepared for tomorrow. It then gives me direction to what I may need to address. There is only one truth and that is LOVE is all there is, this tells me that all else is an illusion. My feeling of anxiety, sadness, grief, worry, separation and all other negativity is a simple indication that I need to address something that is asking to be healed within me. My life is in my own hands and everybody else in it is playing a role to remind me of my own magnificence. I am never stuck, everything is always working for me and through me for my greater good and all those around me. In the past if I made a choice in fear, it would unfold in fear. Today, I do my best to have my thoughts, words and actions be aligned with my core beliefs. I know that all the teachers before me are all saying the same message, but they are simply saying it in their own words just I am doing here now. Those who resonate with me will hear the message of hope, love, courage and bravery in times of sadness and sorrow. These are messages that are capable of healing old wounds, forgiving and releasing old pain, creating much needed space within us for everything that is meant to be for us... a full life of love and adventure.

A few years ago a dear friend of mine, somebody I cared about deeply, mentioned that I made Spirituality look so easy. I smiled at her and said it was one of the hardest things I have had to ever go through, but the most important journey I have ever taken, this journey within. This life, all of us here to support us, I am so happy to be a student of it. I am grateful to be a part of the collective healing. I am humbled to be the mother of 3 children who will see the world differently than the way I was raised. My children will see everything as an adventure and to trust that the Universe is here to support us and Spirit is always here to give us Divine Guidance in Divine timing. To trust in something, we may not be able to see, but to know with blind faith that everything is always good even when things are falling apart. I trust that every roadblock in my life, leads me to a lesson about myself, bringing me closer to the truth of who I really am, love. I believe that when there is a problem, that the solution is also always there, that I only have to choose to ask for help or to see it through the eyes of love.

Today, I choose love over fear. Today, I choose to stay calm and trust. Looking back, I know for a fact, that I am stronger than I ever thought. Going forward I can lean into love, know the truth, and trust that I will be led to the right and perfect people, places and things in my journey.

My prayer for you is that you realize that you too, are stronger than you think, that all the roadblocks in your life are simply a detour into the right direction. May you expand into love, abundance and success with love, joy, grace and ease. Now, go out there and live fully, love deeply and be yourself. You don't have to be anybody else, just the person you were meant to be.

April Nicolas I AM, a mother of three beautiful children, a partner and best friend to the most wonderful man who is perfect for me. I live one day at a time knowing that I am being led daily to the best version of myself. I am a student of life, truth seeker, truth teller, debunker of BS and an avid supporter of living fully. I am committed to sharing tools with others who are ready to step into their greatness by facing their fears, sharing their mess as their message and living their lives as proof. Love is all there is.

Mali Phonpadith

Infinite Souls

Laos, the land of my birth, occupies the heart of Central Southeast Asia. It is quiet in its demeanor, yet resilient and proud. Beneath the surface of natural beauty and graceful people is a history of grief, unhealed wounds and hidden landmines.

Laos is the homeland I fled with my family at the tender age of four, half asleep, in the dark of night, across the Mekong River. When I was born in 1975, the Vietnam War had been officially declared over but it still raged in Laos. My family lived in the city of Thakhek, in the Khammouane province. Khammouane is located in the center of the country, in the upper half of the panhandle over which so much devastation was spread, with the Vietnam boarder to its east. The North Vietnamese army established the infamous Ho Chi Minh Trail here as a route for supplies and troops. This caused the sky to rain bombs.

From the air, the United States conducted massive warfare as they apparently tried to stop the spread of communication. According to The Guardian, "Laos was hit by an average of one B-52 bomb load every eight minutes, 24 hours a day, between 1964 and 1973." That's more bombs than were dropped in all of World War II, giving my homeland the distinction of being the most heavily-bombed country in the world. Eighty million of these bombs failed to explode and now rest, half buried and lethal, in farmlands, hillsides and forests. Despite the biggest bombing campaign in world history, the effort failed to prevent the Communist Party from defeating the royal monarchy of Laos, the kingdom of Lan Xang, which means, "Land of a Million Elephants."

Before the Pathet Lao regime took over, my father worked for the royal government of Laos as a humanitarian. Therefore, he and his colleagues were prime targets. They were blacklisted and my father burned all documents linking him to the old government. He buried his uniform and prayed he would not be discovered.

My father, like so many others who had been unable to flee the country early on, was eventually interned in a remote, disease-ridden camp for "re-education." Had the guards known of his close affiliation with the previous government, he would most likely have been killed. The re-education camps were called samana and their purpose was to break the will of the old regime in all men. My father was in and out of samana for a couple of months. What he witnessed there would haunt him for the rest of his life.

When he was not being "re-educated", he dedicated all of his time to plotting our escape. Along with my grandmother and mother, he had three very young daughters and a son (who was still inside my mother's womb) to consider in this grand exodus. It took three years, but through secret letters and encrypted telegrams to relatives living in Thailand, my father was able to coordinate and execute and escape plan.

We went in the middle of the night, escaping with only the moonlight, and made it across the Mekong River. We came to shore at the exact coordinates that my father had spent years mapping out. Relatives who were living in Thailand met us and hid us in a produce truck, stacking boxes of vegetables to hide us. When we reached a safe house, we stayed with these relatives for a couple of weeks while my father and uncles mapped out a way to get us inside a nearby overcrowded refugee camp.

On the night we traveled to the refugee camp, we quietly waited until there were no guards in sight. My grandmother recounted how she, along with my father and uncle, shoveled dirt underneath barb wired fences so that we could each crawl under and find refuge within the "walls" of the camp. Our family was very fortunate. We lived at the refugee camp for only a year before we were sponsored by Davies Unitarian Church, a small church in the State of Maryland that helped us become permanent residents of the United States of America.

Within that same year of arrival, our church friends helped us rent an apartment and my father was able to find work at a nearby car dealership. Since he did not speak English, the only job he qualified for was the janitor position. He was ecstatic to have work and the opportunity to earn money and support his family. While he appreciated the immense generosity we had experienced from the church members, my father worked hard to reclaim his sense of independence. He wanted to earn his own way and no longer wished to rely on the church or government food stamps.

My mother found work at a local bakery within walking distance from our apartment. She only qualified for the dishwasher position, again due to her lack of English. A year later, she found work as a hotel housekeeper at the J.W. Marriott in Washington, D.C. where she worked for more than 30 years. My father also took on odd jobs like painting fences, mowing lawns and what-ever else he could do to earn extra money on all the days he had off of his full-time janitorial position.

In 1987, seven years after we moved to the United Sates and with their minimum wage jobs, my parents put a down payment of $20,000 in cash to buy our first single family home. We grew up with very little and yet we never felt poor. My grandmother, father and mother, through their actions, showed us how to accomplish the impossible. Owning their home was symbolic. They were able to build a loving home in a new land while living with the permanent wounds of war.

During my childhood days, life was confusing. At home I was a traditional Lao girl and when I went to school, I often found myself either hiding or trying very hard to fit in. I wanted so much to be a typical "American girl." Our parents could not help with homework nor help us navigate the "normal" way of life in American society. They were just as lost as we were. We lived in a town called Upper Marlboro where there were just a few Asian families. Most of our neighbors were African Americans or Latinos, which made it very difficult for us to blend in with our peers.

Identity was a struggle during this phase of my life. By the time I reached middle school, I was tired of living inside my Asian body, so I figured out how to "disguise" myself. I cherished my heritage, but for a budding teenager, it was exhausting to wake up every day knowing somebody would remind me what I looked like and how weird and different I was because of it.

Unfortunately, my ethnicity wasn't the only thing that made me stand out or made me a target of being bullied. I was often ridiculed for being a teacher's pet and called a "nerd" for getting good grades. I wanted to be invisible, but my peers always found a way to call me out. I felt like an outsider and I tried to find any way possible to fit in. So much so, that when I was 13 years old, and still very naïve, I spent every weekend that summer playing in my father's garden working on getting a dark tan.

I was going to a new school that fall season and thought if I tanned long enough, I would fit in with the other black kids, who at that time, made up about 85 percent of our student body. As silly as it sounds now looking back, I was on a mission to create a brand new identity. My mother would tell me to put on sun block, but there was no way I was going to deter the sun from darkening me up!

It was like a race, and I only had three months until the start of the new school season to "become black." While I didn't get the rock star reception I had hoped for, I did make friends that school year. For a while, I attributed the success of my budding friendships and the feeling of acceptance to my new look. And then, one autumn morning, over a weekend, I looked into the mirror and realized, with a surge of panic, that my tan was fading! I became fearful in that moment. What if my façade fell away and my friends discovered that I was in fact Asian? I did not want to go back to a world where no one wanted to be near me, where no one saw me as a human being and where I was constantly being bullied and ridiculed. I cried and then braced myself to be snubbed that following Monday when I arrived back at school.

But all my friends greeted me as usual. I was beyond relieved that they did not notice my skin becoming lighter as winter approached. In fact, as the year went on, they greeted me the same way every day, throughout all the seasons I knew them. Looking back, I think the confidence I gained from feeling like I looked like everyone else primed my inner beauty so that it radiated outwards and drew people into my own light. And all the while, I thought it was my darker skin that made me so appealing. Once I started to focus on my relationship and who I was being, honoring my inner treasures, rather than my outside appearance, my anxiety began to fade away— little by little. Eventually, I no longer worried about the color of my skin determining whether others wanted to be a part of my life. Such early lessons are essential to how we operate as adults.

When I was fifteen years old, I began working at a fast food restaurant to support my parents with household bills. Every other check went to the family expenses and what I was able to keep was in preparation for my college tuition. I worked every night after high school, including weekends, knowing that this was the only way I could afford college. I studied very hard with full intention of qualifying for academic scholarships and eventually graduated at the top of my class. My high marks awarded me several scholarships, covering the first two years of my University tuition.

In order to graduate, I worked full-time, studying very late into the early mornings with only a few hours of sleep each night. This went on for five years. When I finally graduated, it was one of the proudest moments of my life. I witnessed the pure relief and joy in my parent's eyes. I graduated magna cum laude, with degrees in International Business, Marketing and Spanish. After five years of college, I left feeling accomplished and ready to take on the world. Every goal I had ever set, every plan I created in my head, all came true at that moment. I learned then that if I wanted to reach my goals, I had to set intentions and take the daily steps necessary to manifest them into reality.

Two months from college graduation, I was hired by a government contractor to join their commercial marketing division. At age 22, I would be responsible for submitting a marketing plan to the Vice President for consideration. In preparation for this project, I was introduced to a gentleman named Chris, who was part of the federal marketing team. I shared an office with him and he became my friend and mentor. After working closely together for months on end, our friendship blossomed into admiration, which then turned into love. He was a kind and sensitive soul whose laughter was infectious. He was the life of the party and had charisma like you wouldn't believe. It was this natural charm and humor that attracted me to him. Five years flew by and he finally proposed marriage.

On a hot summer day in 2003, Chris and I went on a family picnic. I was excited to introduce him to my extended family and friends as my new fiancé. It was during this picnic that my world came to a halt. As I was finishing up with food preparations, I walked toward the water to see that Chris and my brother-in-law were waist high in the Potomac River, talking and laughing while our nephews and relatives were splashing water at each other. Within seconds, Chris must have felt my presence from afar because he turned around and waved at me. He motioned for me to join them but I held up five fingers, as I still needed a few minutes to finish up with the food prep. He nodded as if to say, "OK" and gave me a thumbs up signal. I smiled, waved and made my way toward the picnic tables. That was the last gesture he ever offered me, telling me he was going to be ok. Soon after I walked away from the scene, there was a riptide that came in and swept away the five of the boys who were wading in the water. My brother-in-law and Chris swam out to rescue them. They were able to bring four to safety with help from nearby jet skiers. Unfortunately, Chris lost his life trying to save the last child, my brother-in-law's nephew, and they both left this earthly plane together that afternoon.

The months that followed, the steps that I took, the weight of an elephant that showed up to sit upon my chest, these things gave me many words with which to fill up my journals. My family and friends were there to support me and yet I needed to find other ways to grieve and to heal from within. I felt so smothered by care and love that I just wanted to be left alone. I didn't want to pretend to be all right. I didn't want to have to shed (or hide) tears. I just wanted to "be" and I was frustrated every day because I didn't know what "being" meant in my despair.

It was at least eight months before I could see or think straight and another year before I fully reached acceptance that my life had taken a different course than the one I had set out to travel. I had to come to terms with this reality and create a fresh starting point. As I embarked on creating a new start, it included a change in my career. I started a financial practice with the goal of educating others on the importance of planning, helping them prepare for unexpected life events like the one I had just experienced.

At my first networking event after launching the practice, I remember feeling nervous and very much alone. There was a moment when I thought to myself, "What am I doing? I have no idea how to run a business. Is building this practice even going to work?" I thought to leave the networking event and just go home, curl up in my bed and cry. But then I heard another voice in my head say; "You have no other choice but to move on with your life. He cannot come back and the only place for you to turn is forward." I took in a deep breath, drew out a sigh and challenged myself to stay. I rallied my inner thoughts to focus. I challenged myself to find the first friendly face that walked through the doors, look forward and go make a new friend.

Several people walked in and then I spotted a man who entered the room with a smile. I remember looking down at his hand and when I spotted a wedding ring, I was certain he was the one to approach. It was safe. He was married and there would be no room for misunderstanding. I went for it. I walked up to him, learned that his name was Victor, and told him that this was my first time at this networking event. I learned it was his first time also. We navigated the room together that day and stayed in touch. He and his wife became clients of mine. As the years went by, we met twice a year for seven years to discuss his financial goals. We became good friends, like so many of my other clients. Victor, however, would become more than a friend. He became (and perhaps always was) a soul mate.

Three years after Chris' passing, we learned that my father had aggressive liver cancer. Within three weeks of learning of his illness, he passed away. I spent every possible hour with my father in those final weeks. I learned so much about this man and his vision and mission for his life. He told me that the moment he got his entire family safely across the Mekong River was the moment he had accomplished his life's mission. Everything else was an additional blessing that he negotiated with the Universe. When he prayed for us to survive that original journey, he promised he'd raise us to be incredible souls. My father did not fear the afterlife; he only worried whether his family members were going to navigate through life without too many challenges.

My journey of grief and healing included other experiences after Chris and my father. Within a timespan of ten years, I dealt with the loss of my godfather to cancer, best friend, Rafael, to suicide, uncle to lung cancer, and grandmother to a decline in health after two hip surgeries. I also had to care for my mother after a full knee replacement and am currently on a journey with my sister as she bravely battles cancer.

What I have come to understand about life's tragic events is that we will all experience them. With each painful setback, we also get setup for a higher level of awareness and consciousness that prepares us for how we handle future challenges. I have found some solace in knowing that we, as human beings, have the capacity to move forward. We can find within us the will and strength to nurture and heal the broken pieces. In fact, we have the ability to regenerate the missing parts of our shattered spirits. It simply takes the desire, the hope, guidance and faith that there is a purpose for our existence. There is a reason why we are here, experiencing what is thrown at us and overcoming the impossible.

I used to think that perhaps I was bad luck. I was afraid to get too close to people for fear that something horrible might happen to them and I would continue to grieve their losses. This has turned out to be an illusion based on my deep fear of loss. I have had to see, own, articulate and release this reality and continue to find healthy ways of letting go of such a crippling fear.

I sought help by reading books, getting counseled, working with transformational coaches, attending retreats, practicing energy modalities such as EFT (emotional freedom technique), seeking support from Reiki practitioners, learning meditation and releasing my emotions through my writing and poetry. For years I went on this journey to free myself of worry, anxiety, insomnia, and an unwillingness to open my heart to loving or being loved.

It took several years before I could tap into a "lightness of being", which I had never experienced before, not even as a child. It was only then, when my spirit felt more awake and free; where I was able to make decisions based on love, hope and abundance versus lack and scarcity. When this moment of clarity arrived, I knew that it would take daily practice to stay calm on a consistent basis. I was 36 years old when I was finally able to tap into these feelings and able to live with trust and faith that "All is as it should be, or it would be something else."

I had allowed romance to enter my life after Chris died but I know now that throughout my dating life, I was still operating on fear, which meant that I was not offering the best version of myself to these wonderful men who wanted to be a part of my world. They each, in their own unique way, taught me that my heart had the capacity to love again, and that I still had a lot of healing work yet to do.

I mentioned that I uncovered a feeling of lightness at the age of 36. That year, 2011, with the advice of my managing partner and peers, I left my financial practice. I decided to launch my own company and help small and midsize businesses get their unique message and mission out into the market. The company has grown into what is now the SOAR Community Network. In that same year I published my memoir, A Million Fireflies, and co-authored a business workbook, Seen and Sustained, with three female entrepreneurs. That July I traveled to Spain for one month to participate in a friends wedding and allowed myself my first vacation in seven years. When I came back to the U.S. I learned that my home, through a bank error, was sold at auction, which led to a civil law suit and forced me start all over again.

During this same tumultuous yet liberating time, Victor, yes the gentleman I met eight months after losing Chris, called me to share that he had separated from his wife. He was living with an old childhood friend from Puerto Rico, and wanted to start writing and playing music. He knew that I was a poet and that I had collaborated with a friend on writing songs. On that call he was very honest in sharing that he was trying to uncover his own gifts and talents to create ways of healing and moving forward with his life. Besides his work as a technology expert, he shared that the only other constant in his life was his love of music. He asked if I wanted to meet his roommate and join them in writing original songs. I gladly accepted because it would be the perfect distraction from the pending lawsuit.

A year after we started the band, our feelings for one another grew but neither of us truly knew when it had turned from friendship into love. It slowly happened and it grew through our shared values and vision for life. As complex as it was, both understanding that he was still in the midst of a separation, there was a knowing that we would be fine regardless of what direction our friendship needed to take. We both agreed that peace had to be a part of the equation.

As fate would painfully have it, the same week that he and his wife submitted their divorce papers, she was diagnosed with Leukemia and within 8 months she passed away peacefully with her loved ones, including Victor, by her side.

Life is full of unexpected twists and turns. It offers so many contradictions including pain and joy, hatred and love, light and dark, life and death. I have come to learn that our life experiences, especially the most painful ones, create an empathy bucket that stretches far and wide. Because I truly understood what happens to a human heart when you lose someone you love, I was able to support Victor on his personal journey of loss and healing. It made us grow closer. I got him. He got me. This newly, yet unwanted experience, bonded and solidified our friendship. Today he is my best friend, husband, business partner, and life companion. He accepts my humanness and knows the purity of my soul like no other on this planet.

When I am asked to share my story, whether through a publication like Born to Be Me, on stage, or during interviews, I often wonder what parts to share. Do I leave out the painful events so that others don't feel heavy and sad? Do I focus only on the triumphant and blissful moments? The more I am asked to share, the more I realize that the audience wants to connect to another human being who hurts, bleeds, loves and dreams like they do.

The meaning of the word story, according to Dictionary.com is "an account of past events in someone's life or in the evolution of something." This definition reminded me that our full stories include all the moments that contribute to designing our ever-evolving persons. When I was born, I came with a package, predesigned by a lineage of countless evolving souls. When we tell our stories, we are sharing a collection of infinite moments that have led each of us to this exact time and place, in this very lifetime.

Storytelling has been one of the unifying ways for our ancestors to evolve and thrive as a civilization. Although we have not always used our words, knowledge and power for good as a collective society, we have the capabilities to do so. When we share our stories from an honest and vulnerable place, we open up gateways for understanding. These gateways will be what lead us to more compassion and harmony in the world.

For Born to Be Me, I decided to share both the pains and joys of life because I want to create a gateway to those who have experienced tragedies and traumas. I want them to know that they have a fellow human being who understands the depth of their pain, who has felt the isolation and frustration that they may have felt or perhaps currently feel.

I am also here to remind them that life does move forward and that walking toward the light does often take painful steps. I am asking them to trust that one day they'll arrive at the end of the dark tunnel. In time, they will be greeted with new blessings and lessons that will add to the width and depth of their empathy bucket. The experiences contained inside that "bucket" will become the reservoir they'll draw from when they realize and accept that some of greatest roles they'll ever play in this life include friend, lover, teacher, and light bearer.

If you're out there and are feeling alone, remember to look up into the sky and trust that there are infinite souls who see you, have experienced what you feel and are shining their light upon you. There will come a time when other souls will be looking up at you and drawing hope and inspiration from your life experiences and the lasting contributions you offered when you were here, living on this earthly plane.

Mali Phonpadith is the Founder and CEO of the SOAR Community Network (SCN), author, speaker, marketing strategist, podcaster and the Executive Producer of Tea with Mali. In 2015, Mali was selected as a Belief Team community partner through Values Partnership for the Oprah Winfrey's OWN Network BELIEF initiative.

She is the Founder of SCN Leadership Breakfast and the host of the SCN SOAR Podcast (Named New and Noteworthy and What's Hot on iTunes in 2014). A Million Fireflies is Mali's memoir about her voyage from war-torn Laos to America.

Dr. Kim Redman

The Magic of Passion and Purpose

I'm having a gratitude moment. It's a glorious Florida night filled with gentle breezes, and tropical flora. The singer looks at me and says "This is for you." Suddenly Frank Sinatra's "I Did It My Way" is wafting through the air, as my father looks over at me across the table of our authentic Italian restaurant and laughs out loud. "Well, Number One", he says, using the nickname of our birth order, (and yes I am the first child), "there couldn't be a song better suited to you."

True enough. But boy, did I do it the hard way! Abandonment, death by strangulation (I came back), a cervical spine injury that left a hairline crack in C2 and ligament damage, cervical cancer, rehabbing for a year to learn how to walk again, and other injuries too numerous to list. There certainly was an easier way, and I would venture there were many more elegant ways to learn some of the lessons of my journey.

NATURE OF TRUTH

I work with the Ray of Truth as it is known in esoteric and quantum circles. It turns me into a bit of a human lie detector and it took a lot of training to figure out when someone is lying to themselves vs. someone intentionally lying to me. It's a very useful tool as a Master Results Coach. As one of my esoteric teachers said, "The truth may set you free, but first it's going to kick your ass." Truth seems like such a simple concept in the abstract. Once you begin to address truth at the level of the individual, we are no longer speaking about an abstract truth; we are speaking about perception. Perception is subjective, and as such, it changes.

The truth is, that I was a loved and planned child. The truth is, that my parents loved me very much. The truth is, that they did the best they knew how to do with the tools that they had been given and discovered along the way. It is a truth that my parents wanted my sister and I to be happy. The truth is, that my parents desperately hoped to create a joyful family. My dad would often say that he wanted us to be like the TV show, "The Waltons."

Other truths exist in this same space. It is also a truth, that my mother spent her whole life attempting to come to terms with a dysfunctional, turbulent, and psychologically toxic relationship with her own mother. Often an all or nothing dynamic, I witnessed duty warring with self preservation, and the toll of that wild pendulum swing. The truth is that the unbalanced nature of my grandmother and mother's relationship, poured out onto the relationship my mother had with me. The truth is, that the toxic and violent patterns from one generation moved into the present generation with my mother and I.

The truth was that I could see where the pattern was leading and I desperately needed to find a way out.

As a young woman, it became clear to me that I was going to do it all differently (feel free to swoon with drama, adding your hand to your forehead as you say this). Being right was the original religion in my family. Coming from a Mediterranean descent meant that being right was often determined by who was loudest and sharpest, verbally. Doing it differently, began with rejecting all the lessons from my maternal line, and that was my first step in continuing the all or nothing pattern of my childhood.

I had to find out how this crazy dynamic was created and how I could change it. The shamans I have worked with have taught me that I created the intensity of my lessons as a type of initiation onto my healer and leader path. Unconsciously of course. A much older and wiser self would come to know that the real dynamic that my mother and grandmother were fighting over was about power and value, and the core lessons of being enough.

Truth Lesson ONE:

All or nothing always fails because it is a win-lose dynamic. With a win-lose dynamic you have an opponent, not a partner. With this dynamic one person wins and the other person is resentful. The relationship always loses. In order to have a successful relationship, the relationship itself needs to come out on top. It's a win-win-win dynamic. The reality check is that this win-win-win requires a choice where happy, healthy and wealthy is more important to you than being right. It's tough on the ego to start, but glorious in its ability to produce sustainable and empowering results.

Truth Lesson TWO:

Here's what leaders and successful people know: It takes a tribe to thrive. Independence doesn't mean doing it all alone.

Independence means being able to be self sufficient and also being able to resource and interface with a team. No man is an island. It takes a village to raise a child. These are not platitudes. Alone equals a very low glass ceiling. Alone is not sustainable. Alone means that you cannot lead or be led to success.

Truth Lesson THREE:

You are enough. I am enough. We are enough. Enough is not something you earn, it is something you own as your birthright. I believe that this lesson is essential to the well-being of our species. If we seek to heal the disempowerment pandemic, we need to change our focus, our dialogue, and the stories we share. Can we honor ourselves as Goddesses, and the men in our lives as Gods? Can we find the sacred within ourselves and by finding that truth, find it others? Are we willing to take that journey of intimacy? Within this authenticity, can we reach out and create a deep Sisterhood that stretches beyond the 'mean girl' dynamic of our pre-teen youth? I say that the answer is an emphatic, YES!

PASSION AND PURPOSE

I always say that your passion will lead you to your purpose. Cautionary note: Passion is a fuel. Like all fuel it can launch a spacecraft, or blow up on the launch pad. As I rejected the traditional lessons of womanhood and family, I followed my heart.

I was seeking! Seeking freedom from the constraints I brought with me. Seeking to escape my own internal programming. Seeking to "make change." (What change this was I had no idea - but I believed then that wanting it was enough. It's not, by the way). I was seeking affirmation externally that I was good enough, or worth enough, to belong to a tribe, after the abandonment of my family. I was seeking answers as to how these scenarios could have happened to a loved, planned child. I was seeking how to heal and change the world.

In reality, I was seeking how to heal and change me, but I didn't know that consciously at the time. My Higher Self, the Divine, and it seemed the Universe, were in on the plan. They assisted me in creating the perfect situations to reveal the answers that I was seeking. The answers needed unwrapping though, and that took some time.

I found inconvenient truths, and profound depths of self while professionally studying theater, and later in touring (including Shakespeare in the Park). I was known for taking on deep, conflicted characters and portraying them with uncomfortable authenticity. I would lose myself for weeks in a character, and the character itself would provide the structure I needed to stay safe psychologically. What I found while deep diving into the dark places of the psyche was a place of stillness in the midst of the chaos, and in that stillness, I found me. Every time I came through one of these performances or runs, I would be exhausted, yet sated. Every time I came back, I traveled back with a piece of me that I thought had been lost in the family wounding. Intuitively guided, psycho-drama therapy! Who knew?

I found the mechanics and structure of the psyche while studying developmental psychology. The need to know how to change my family drama, led me to change what I went to university for. Originally I wanted to study languages, as I had a natural proclivity for them that I figure came to me via genetics and nurturing. My parents both had English as a second language. I had hoped to work with the United Nations and get paid to travel as I translated. Great plan! Not happening.

Developmental psychology, psycholinguistics, abnormal psychology and the psychology of learning, all taught me how the damage had happened. I learned how dysfunctional patterns had been brought forward generationally, but not how to change those patterns. Later on, I would learn how the tools of the unconscious mind were the right tools for that job, and I studied them intensively. Research and statistics primed me to run the live research study that brought my doctoral thesis to life over 20 years later, founding Quantum Leadership™ internationally. No one was more shocked than I was to find I had put together something new.

Having theater and psychology in my tool belt positioned me for one of the greatest gifts of my life, although I didn't know it at the time. The theater that I was under contract with was chosen to work with the city of Buffalo on pilot project called "The Chapter One Program." This project went into three at-risk schools, and targeted students whom the system was failing. These were the most at-risk students, and in some of the worst neighborhoods. With almost no budget we were to mastermind how to use the performing arts, as a 'whole-body' learning mechanism, to see if we could shift the students test scores against the national averages. We didn't just shift them. We blew those scores away. So much so that the Governor of the State of New York invited us all to go to the mansion for a celebratory dinner.

I had found my calling. Holding space for the transformation that comes at the moment we release our victim story and remember our Magnificence. Watching kids who had given up, and been given up on by age ten, recover their pride, their belief in themselves and decide that they could do anything, changed my life. It was a bigger rush than a standing ovation of 5,000 people! I had a six-year-old give me my job description; "Miss Kim, it's your job to believe, so hard, that we are magic, that we remember to believe it ourselves. You use the BIG magic, love." That is the life moment when I understood that I really could make a difference. It still brings tears of gratitude 30 years later and it still fuels my both my personal mission, and the company mission.

One of my first signs that someone else found this work important was the moment I received the call from the Lincoln Centre Arts in Education program. They wanted me to go forward into other schools. It was powerful. It was frustrating especially when coming up against the status quo. It was also exciting when like minds came together. It taught me about synergy, where we are more than the sum of our parts. I learned that together we were more, could do more, could be more.

Following a boyfriend on a dare, led me to paramedicine, where I found the physiological mechanisms of trauma, and how to work with them. Transforming the symptomology of trauma and PTSD is one of things I am known for today, and we do a lot of give-back with returning soldiers. I also learned that 'the hip bone was in fact connected to the thigh bone' as the childhood song goes. The physical science assisted me in becoming a better healer, again, years later. In hindsight it seems I was taking life courses that would prepare me for my real mission. My friends all said, "Can't you do, just one thing?" The answer at the time was no. I was too busy picking up the pieces I would need later on.

The value of self-worth was perhaps the hardest set of lessons. Those lessons came in the form of an emotional and sexually abusive relationship. In the quantum world we teach that "energy in motion = emotion." The bigger the emotion, the bigger the energy. Abuse produces big energy, and ultimately that was used for transformation. In the depths of despair, I found the gift of my Inner Goddess. The Goddess relationship is still one of the most important relationships in my life and it continues to evolve as I evolve. It is compassionate, heart-based, and sustainable. It also requires saying no, without apology, anger, or explanation. That too is a powerful gift.

Passionate Lesson ONE:

Using our feelings as evidence that we are, or are not, on the right track, is lethal. Our feelings will give us data about where our lives are out of balance. For example, if we are angry all the time, something is out of balance. Our job is to find what's out of balance and change that, rather than reinstalling our anger by talking about our anger ad nauseam. We are designed to use results as evidence that we are on track. Healthy humans feel all of their emotions, and those emotions shift constantly depending on what movie we are playing in our head. Results keep us authentic, sustainable, and give us a funnel to pour our passions into.

Passionate Lesson TWO:

I now know that self-worth requires a set of skills. These skills allow passion to be a safe and sustainable fuel. They include the three step process of boundary setting, the four stages of learning and social development, self-sourcing, and the ability to say, "No." No is a full sentence, by the way. Really. Say it while smiling. It's fun!

Passionate Lesson THREE:

Your passion will lead you to your purpose. The nature of your purpose won't be self evident until you have journeyed down the path for a bit. Hindsight is 20/20. It will make sense in the end, but not at the beginning of the path. You have to agree to take the journey, to get the magic and benefits of that journey. You don't need to know what's at the end of the journey. You do need to commit the first step, every day. It's just a decision, so make a decision. You can course correct afterwards. The bicycle will always fall down unless it is in motion.

QUANTUM REALITY

I learned the hard way that we are "God-spark." We create our realities according to all esoteric, philosophy, mysticism, and quantum physics. As I like to say from the stage, "Welcome to Life School. It's called Planet Earth University. How's it going so far?"

For me I created the big "C", and while I was waiting for my very kind doctor to remove a large section of my plumbing, he suggested that I explore the power of the mind.

Another beautiful unfolding occurred under the guise of team development while I was working on an ambulance. Our annual gala always reminded me of a prom. Whereas earlier in the day, my teammates (almost all of whom were men) would let a door slam on me while I was carrying oxygen tanks, in my dress they would hold my chair. In their defense they would say, "But you're a girl now! Before you were one of us." In their own convoluted way, it was a compliment. At this event, our team leader was setting up a rock climbing and repelling practice session. I was always interested, and he really wanted me to be there to lead the way for the other young women on our unit. I agreed to go.

Have you ever said, "Wow! What was I thinking?!" I said it the next morning as I was safely harnessed in, hanging over the ledge, 100 feet over the path of the whirlpool in the Niagara Gorge park. When you repel you can't simply step off the ledge because you are standing on a flat surface (the ground) and have to wind up with your feet on a surface that is 90 degrees in difference (the wall). You need to leap. Literally. The metaphor of my life, it seems. Success meant being supported while leaping, literally, into the unknown.

When you repel there is always a 'belay' person, who in essence acts as a backup safety for you. About ten feet down the wall, I realized there was no safety person. Seconds later, a stranger grabbed the rope and guided me down the wall. His name was Steven and he was part lawyer, and part shaman. That was the first time he saved my life that day.

The second time Steven saved my life that day was during my first ascent while rock climbing. Again, Steven was acting as my belay person, and as I was hanging onto a ledge about 70 feet in the air, the ledge broke off leaving me swinging in the air. He interrupted my scream with a yelled question, "How's the view?!" The view? It was spectacular! Awe inspiring. Humbling. Who gets to soak in a view that unique?

Needless to say this formed some trust between us. Enough trust that when he asked me later on why I had created my cancer, and what I needed to learn from it, I refrained from throwing him into the gorge (although I did briefly think about it.)

For that summer, rock climbing taught me how to focus exclusively on the next step in front of me, and on the result I wanted. Steven taught me how to safely explore the quantum world of my inner self and held my hand, as I set boundaries in the outer world. Nutritionists taught me that the body needed building blocks and I entered the world of nutraceuticals; pharmaceutical levels of vitamins and minerals.

It was a summer of learning that everything is connected. It is holographic; what impacts one thing, impacts them all. It changed my paradigm, my world view, and set me firmly on the path of Quantum Integrative Science, long before it was ever called that. At the end of the summer a miracle occurred. I was lucid dreaming in the wee hours of the morning, floating inside my body. I was Light, and there were other Light beings/particles around me. While I watched, the last of the cancer was literally blasted away. My whole tribe had that same dream that morning, and when I went for my pre-surgical check I was informed that the cancer had 'spontaneously remissed'. My surgeon said that he didn't want to know exactly what I had done, and that he was quite proud of me for doing it.

I rock climbed as my main sport for several years after this, all over the eastern seaboard of North America, with Steven as my climbing partner. Eventually others took over my quantum training, leading to over 30 years in the Mystery Schools. Steven and I went our own ways, and I kept my promise to him that I would keep learning and pay it forward. I continue to learn and teach the top integrative change modalities, and Ancient Wisdoms. Blessings.

Two years ago there was a study on the top 50 medical studies about how negative emotions, and repressed rage and sadness specifically, were an integral part of how we created disease and how releasing those emotions was an integral part in how we heal. The original studies were done at some of the most prestigious medical institutes in the world, many of which are in North America. All 50 studies contain the same message. I will paraphrase one of my favorite catch phrases, "You gotta get real, about what you feel, if you want to heal."

As we say in Neuro Linguistic Programming (NLP), "Your focus creates your behavior, and your behavior creates your results." Choose wisely. Action to shift what is out of balance and your body and life will follow. That's called an 'actionable focus' in coaching.

Quantum Reality Lesson ONE:

You are a hologram. Quantum physics speculates that the whole Universe is a hologram. This means that everything we think, feel, and do, impacts everything else. It is lunacy to believe that your work-life doesn't impact your home-life and visa versa. It does because it impacts your biology and wherever you go, there you are! This is also how we get the most bang for our buck... any asset we add into the system, benefits the whole system. Everywhere!

Quantum Reality Lesson TWO:

Your biology doesn't "think" about how you feel. Actually it doesn't care what you think at all. It cares what you believe, how you feel, and whether or not you perceive that you have choice in your life. It's the ultimate feedback mechanism. Your biology responds to the environment outside of you, and the environment between your ears.

I would speculate that the world inside your head is even more impactful than the world outside of us, because we carry that inner Universe with us, everywhere. Then we project "the way it is" onto the world around us, creating self-fulfilling prophecies. Life happens. What the meaning we take away, is ours. On her last show, Oprah said something that really stuck with me, "it doesn't matter what your mamma did, or your daddy didn't do. There is no reason to not have the life you want." It made me think about what things I could change. Whatever methods you use, shamanism, NLP, psychology, know that they all work. Please learn the tools to change your inside world. It's the best way to create the world you were born to thrive in.

Quantum Reality Lesson THREE:

You always have choice. If you can't see or hear those choices, if you can't wrap your hands around the fact that there is a choice, then by definition you have a gap. The solution is to reach out to somebody solution-minded and to do that reach out within 48 hours. I will readily admit that in acknowledging those choices you may need to let go of being right, in order to reach happy, healthy and wealthy. Success does breed success. The more, happy, healthy and wealthy we get, the less we care about being right. Set up your outside environment in whatever ways you can to support your happy healthy and wealthy self.

QUANTUM SUCCESS

Tony Robbins like to say that "there are two components to a highly successful life. The art of living joyfully, and the science of living abundantly." Living joyfully is an art because joy is subjective and unique to each of us. Abundance, money and success are all based on a recipe, and skills.

I am a talented person. It took years to build skills. I work with a lot of talented people. Talented people want it all yesterday. In my healing I needed to learn that the shamans say "It is done, when it is done", for a reason.

Talent is the icing. Skill is the cake. You need a recipe to bake a successful cake, and baking is a science. Following the recipe, is more important than your individual genius or intelligence. My mother-in-law makes award winning pastry crust. It is a recipe that her mother-in-law handed down to her. Mom likes to speak about the feel of the dough, and how many batches of dough you need to 'work' in order to get that 'feel'. She reminds me that no one is allowed to change the recipe until they have the feel, and that by the time they have the feel they don't want to change the dough! Use your creativity on the filling and the icing instead.

I needed to surrender; to the Divine, to the process, to the mission of being in service, and that meant surrendering the need to do it alone. Surrender is part of success, and it is still a challenging lesson for me. I know if it's hard, I'm doing it wrong. If I get a result, I am doing it right. It's a pretty simple philosophy, but it doesn't mean it is easy.

Seek out mentorship. Seek out coaches (I work with three mentors now). It makes success a party and gives you a pick me up when it's hard. A good mentor will share with you their secret recipes. We all need someone to guide us around the big potholes, or at least help winch our way out of the hole! Keep asking until it vibes with you. You deserve it.

Right now on planet Earth, we are in a 'bridging time' between science and spirit, between past and future, between the "haves" and the have "nots", and we have the opportunity to create a society that supports us all. This bridging time allows us to synthesize ideologies and concepts, and easily synergize new techniques. Many of our quantum programs came to fruition in support of this flowering and unfolding awareness. It is a special time and I personally invite you to join us on this powerful journey.

Quantum Success Lesson ONE:

All resistance, hardship and obstacles are there because we need to learn something. This something can be a skill set, a behavior, or an ideology that stretches us beyond our comfort zone. Growth begins at the end of the comfort zone. Change is inevitable, and growth is a choice. Your ego will get an initial bashing, and then magic will happen.

Quantum Success Lesson TWO:

Gratitude. The Universe is perfect even if I am not. This means that all things really do happen for a reason. I am the reason, and if I can get the learning and the "aha" then I can move into gratitude. This lesson will make your Universe a much better place to be.

Quantum Success Lesson THREE:

Seek out success recipes. Question the people around you until you find someone who is already successful at what you are seeking to do and achieve. Ask them to mentor you, or coach you, so that you can get their success recipes. This is how to be effective. This method also allows us to get our happy, healthy, and wealthy, so much faster than before.

We are in a place of consciousness evolution and I know now that this is why I was "Born to Be Me." Everything on my seemingly convoluted path, was perfect, and timely. I now know that I am here for a purpose, what that purpose is, and how to stay on the path of that mission, course correcting as necessary.

Stay grounded, and reach for the stars. You deserve it, and the world needs what you have. Thanks for reading my story!

In Love and Light–
Dr. Kim

Dr. Kim Redman is the Visionary of Creatrix Transformational Solutions Inc. and many transformational programs like Designing Your Destiny®, Go Quantum™, and the Journey of Truth™ She is known for her powerful stage presence and is a multiply published author. Dr. Kim has been nominated for Canada's 100 Most Powerful Women and has received the Order of St. John Priory Vote of Thanks for her volunteer work. She is the founding expert of Quantum Leadership™ and the Master Trainer of NLP and Hypnosis, who brought the Fastrak program including Time Line Therapy™ and Results Coaching to Canada. Dr. Kim's world is "Where East Meets West for Quantum Success."

Teresa Scaini

Living Life Looking Through the Lens of Possibility!

A friend of mine once asked me "when will you decide to live your potential? Initially, when I heard those words I had many thoughts running through my mind. I wondered how she could possibly say this, or who was she to make this kind of judgment about me? This friend was someone I really looked up to, admired and respected, to say I was offended was putting it mildly.

This statement began to fester within me. I even looked up the definition of potential in the dictionary, it meant "expressing possibility." I pondered that. Did I see possibilities beyond what I had in my life? And what exactly did she mean by "when will you decide?", how was I responsible for this decision? I had never thought of possibilities, other than what I was living. It took me a while to viscerally wrap my mind around this new concept.

I had always viewed the world from 2 different lenses; people who didn't have to work hard at anything, they seemed to have it all, everything came so easily to them. Then the others— people like myself, working hard at everything and never really feeling like anything was easy. Life as I saw it, was to work hard and just get by. I was raised with these values. The harder I worked the more respected I might be. My parents were great models of this concept. They both came from hard working families. This model of hard work, get by and hope that you are respected had no room for possibilities. It was evident to me, that as an adult, I followed this same model of values and ethics.

My upbringing resulted in living my life in the safe zone, only seeing one way, very much like tunnel vision. I wasn't sure of how I had decided this, who decides that they lack potential or are void of expressing possibilities? As I began to explore and to peel back the layers one by one, I came to understand that we make decisions momentarily in life without being aware of it consciously. Somewhere, at some point, I had decided that I lacked potential and could not see any other possibilities. The question I asked myself was, "what potential did I have?" and "how would I express possibilities"? The more I thought about it, the more I could hear myself come up with many more limitations. It's so easy to hit the glass ceiling in life when you believe you are only capable of working hard and worthy of little success.

In my mind, there was always the two groups of people— the ones that had everything, well, they were smart and intellectual. These people were well read, had great careers, achieved wealth, married wealth and lived in beautiful homes. Life for them was abundant without a care in the world. And then there were the others— people like myself, who came from hard working families, not smart or intellectual and were great at working with their hands in a trade of some sort. These people married the same type of hard working people and any wealth they accumulated stemmed from these values and ethics. Life in my mind, was very much a tunnel vision.

Up until this point, I saw life through the lens of zero possibilities. I absolutely believed deep down, I was not intellectual or smart.

This belief had prevented me from the pursuit of: a university education, working in management, investing my money, getting married and having children earlier in life and so much more. I believed, I was not meant to be prosperous. It was never a thought in my mind that I would one day inspire, lead or empower others. I believed I was unworthy and limited in potential— never seeing anything other than where I was in the moment and never the thought of any possibilities.

It wasn't until years later, I came to understand that this belief was more than just the model and values I had been raised with. As I began my own journey of transformation, going deep and peeling back the layers one by one, I realized it was actually from one specific time and event. I had made a decision, which in turn became a belief, it stemmed back to a time when I was about 8 years old. This memory was so powerful that it resulted in me creating barriers, preventing me from being and doing more in life.

When I began to explore this memory through my Unconscious Mind it took me back to a vivid detailed memory. I remembered clearly being in my classroom and sitting at my desk. I was so far into the memory, I could see myself sitting at my desk, my head bent down and my heart was pounding. I could feel the pencil I was holding in hand, I could smell the classroom and the chalk. I remembered every aspect of the room and I felt like I was transported back to that time.

As I looked toward the front of the room I knew I was in grade 4. I could see my teacher sitting at her desk, papers in front of her with her hands clasped, directly in front of her, sat my mother. They were talking, it was an extensive conversation and I could hear them clearly. I could see how my teacher was giving a detailed account about me. She expressed how I was not able to grasp reading or math. That I was not capable to comprehend these concepts. She stated that, I was struggling, and learning was difficult for me. The words I heard was "she is limited in understanding", that it was best for me to go in the direction of a trade, to work with my hands or get a job in a factory.

I began to remember how much I hated the black board. I heard my name being called to come to the front of the classroom, written on the black board a mathematical equation with instructions to write out the answer. I stood in front of the blackboard for the longest time, writing and erasing just standing there. I could hear whispers behind me of how dumb I was, kids snickering, footsteps coming up behind me with a big sigh, instructions to just go sit down and the look of disbelief on her face. I felt my heart was pounding so hard, my hands were sticky and sweaty and I was biting the inside of my cheek to hold back the tears. As a child, I didn't have the words to describe what I was feeling, I desperately wanted a hole to open and have it swallow me up. As an adult, I describe it as the wound of humiliation.

That parent-teacher meeting resulted in the decision to have me fail grade 4. I was, however, rewarded by repeating the year again with the same teacher resulting in further humiliation. I would love to put a number to the amount of times I stood in front of that blackboard, trying to solve a mathematical equation. Let's just say the routine of humiliation happened daily and each day, I would pray for a hole to open below me and swallow me up. Surviving school became part of my regime.

I lived in my own private world and it was brilliant. My imagination transported me on grand adventures traveling the world, painting in Paris by the Eiffel Tower, having tea in London, riding camels, seeing the pyramids, going to the land down under. I was always somewhere new exploring. Little did I realize one day, I would travel to these places and experience most of the world.

This memory had been dormant within my Unconscious Mind for years, and yet, it was so powerful! It had stopped me from being open to possibilities, prevented my creativity and I was unable to recognize my gifts. I felt angry and had bouts of sadness that I had allowed myself to believe I was unworthy and lacking potential. I felt rage that an educator could make such a clinical decision about my abilities. I was enraged that I was humiliated each day, by a teacher who continually sent me to the blackboard knowing I didn't understand the math concept. I was pissed that as a teacher, she was not invested in my magnificence, nor to find a way for me to learn or explore other methods of teaching. I harbored resentment towards my mother for believing I was not smart— for agreeing to let me repeat the year with the same teacher and for not advocating loudly on my behalf. I felt these negative emotions for a long time. I was angry with everyone around me and mostly myself. How could anyone believe in my potential if I didn't?

Clearly, I knew I was not in a great place. I was good at faking it and when you feel humiliation, less attention is best. I felt that hiding was a great strategy. I desperately wanted to feel good, discover what it meant to be happy, experience joy and have a peaceful mind. I read books and watched leading experts speak of forgiveness and how forgiving was pivotal in finding happiness again. The more I tried to forgive, the angrier I felt, which spiraled into more sadness. I wanted to burst open and be something bigger and greater than I was living. I truly wanted to move out of my rut.

This was around the time when the book and movie, "The Secret" came out and everyone seemed to be on the positivity kick. I had watched "The Secret" and I liked the concept of, think positive, be positive and attract everything you want by visualizing it. What a great concept! Yet, the more I attempted to put this into practice, the harder it became. I was often up in the 'crazy tree' in my mind, attempting to control my thoughts. Obviously, the model of being positive and the laws of attraction worked for many people. I was trying so hard to install a positive attitude in my life, however, I kept spiraling back to anger and sadness. It was very much 2 steps forward and then 1 step back.

I researched who these innovative mentors were on "The Secret", and what were they doing to be successful? This generated a deep appreciation within me that you cannot change how you do what you do consciously. All learning, all change and every behavior is always at the unconscious level. When I came to this realization it was like winning the lottery. It was the secret ingredient to success. All these innovative people were in alignment with their Unconscious Mind. They had gone deep and had broken through the barriers of their limitations.

I was curious and open to learning how I could adapt this into my life. With each step forward came more knowledge and people who guided me onto the most brilliant journey. I began to explore and learn about Neuro Linguistic Programming (NLP) and Hypnosis. This was such a new concept for me, I decided to push past my fear of the unknown, and I immersed myself with the tools to be in rapport with my Unconscious Mind. NLP gave me the tools to push past my deeply rooted belief that I was not smart or intellectual and lacking in potential.

So, how much anger, sadness or rage did I express before I surrendered to claiming my life back? My pain became so great that I couldn't even stand to be around myself, there was nowhere to hide or run to. I couldn't take one more minute of the heavy feeling in my chest. This moved me to dig even deeper within my Unconscious Mind, going to the root of my problem. My mission was to see what my strengths were, how I learned, and what came easily to me. I began to explore how I would begin a journey of potential, growth and a new belief.

Creating this type of change was exciting and yet terrifying. If I didn't believe that I was unworthy, limited in learning and lacking in potential then what was I? I had run the story of working hard and not being smart for years. I was great at telling this story, it was perfectly scripted and well versed. And if I couldn't run the story, then what story did I have? This was a huge "aha moment" in my life, I realized I had been focused on a story that kept me stuck, never moving forward.

Pushing past my fears, I continued moving forward learning beyond the scope of what I knew. I wanted to be intellectual, abundant in all areas of my life and have everything be easy and effortless. It was all up to me. I began to read anything and everything I could get my hands on. Each time I went to the bookstore I became braver and braver choosing books that were more complex. I used the metaphor of grocery shopping — shop only on the outer circle of the store for natural fresh products. I circled the bookstore beyond novels and sought out anything I could learn about. My knowledge began to grow and not surprisingly, I became an avid reader. Somewhere along the way I realized that not only did I love to read, but I decided that I could read and understand what I was reading. My now favorite place where I like to spend time, to recharge my batteries is always in a library or a book store surrounded by pages filled with knowledge.

School had always been a tough place to be, it very much felt like putting in time, I feared it. I had gone to school because it was mandatory, as a young adult I attended a college administrative course so that I had something to show on a resumé. As I expanded my transformational journey, I began making decisions to expand my skills. I immersed myself in learning a third language, Spanish, and within a year, I was speaking fluently and at ease in conversation. Part of studying the language was submerging myself in the culture, I spent months away in a Latin country volunteering and teaching English. These memories are forever part of my journey of change, it moved me to becoming the person I really wanted to be, and moved me to create the belief of expressing possibilities.

All these steps lead me to becoming a Master Coach and Trainer of Neuro Linguistic Programming (NLP) and Hypnosis. I recall when I took the plunge and made the decision to become an NLP Practitioner. Initially I still doubted that I would be successful in understanding the training or writing the test. Deep down, I still felt the nagging feeling or heard myself wondering if I could do it. It was at this point, that I was really on my way to evolving into my higher self.

I blew out my limiting beliefs of the past and created new beliefs that I learned easily and effortlessly through my Unconscious Mind. I decided that I could simply use all the tools for myself and as a Coach to empower, inspire and lead others. The more I applied what I learned and made it part of my everyday life, the easier it was for me to stand in my power. This lead ultimately to becoming a Trainer of NLP and Hypnosis, I smile when I think of this, as it was never a possibility I could see in the past.

Shortly after I had completed my first level of NLP Practitioner Training, a family member asked me "isn't it hard for you to forgive this"? I had expended time and energy, deeply rooted in this belief, years spent blaming the school system, my teacher, my mother and myself. NLP taught me that humans act and behave based on what they know and the resources they have. Wow, this was a completely foreign theory to me, there was no forgiveness needed. This was freedom to me and deeper than any form of forgiveness. I felt complete gratitude knowing that everyone in my family, or anyone I had a connection with, was also acting and making decisions with the knowledge they had.

Remember the story I would tell about my limitations and how I lacked in potential? Each time I told the story of all my limitations the deeper the belief became rooted within me. I decided that I too, must be accountable for my actions and begin a new story. I could speak of my past without bringing up every single detail and immersing myself back in pain and blame. This new way of telling my story left me empowered, like a big weight lifted off my shoulders. All the stress and pressure I had been holding onto for years, now released.

I also surrendered to the realization that I was ultimately responsible for my results. I had exhausted years, speaking of pain and blame and now what story would I say? My journey was all about creating a mindset of accountability, I was ultimately responsible good or bad for what I had accomplished. I mean all of it! Being responsible for all my choices, decisions and actions. There was no one to blame, only the surrender that I had acted and made decisions with the knowledge I had.

As a Coach working with clients, I can appreciate how easily a decision can become a belief. Beliefs become crippling and debilitating and the deeper they are rooted, the more anger, sadness, fear, anxiety we experience. I decided that I would speak of only my success, potential and a world of new possibilities. I began the new story of how my past had me deeply rooted in a belief lacking potential and now I learn easily and am limitless in potential.

I understood how I had blocked my potential and closed myself off from seeing any possibilities. When I opened myself to envisioning and exploring, wow, the tunnel vision expanded beyond what I thought possible. In retrospect, this was clearly a decision on my part. I decided to be infinite in my potential and have my Unconscious Mind show me possibilities. Now, I got the big picture of how these mentors had become successful by using their tools. They had dealt with their limitations, they believed in their potential and they could see possibilities. Their focus determined their behavior and their behavior determined their results.

An important part of my journey of change was to begin the most prominent relationship of my life, a relationship with myself. I knew that I must court myself, allow alignment within and make this relationship a priority. I had begun a big cleanup of limiting decisions and beliefs, created wholeness within, and deciphered how I was wired. This digging was like a courtship. Like a courtship, you begin to find out how to make the courtship blossom into a wonderful relationship. Investing my time and energy into myself resulted in breaking through barriers, believing everything was possible. I made this relationship with myself, primary.

My past has been a powerful tool to bring forward with me. Learning from this experience was painful, humiliating and yes, I held onto it for a long time. The true power was in what I learned, this was priceless. I recall when I met my husband, he was everything I had really wanted, I somehow manifested this wonderful man. He had qualities from both groups of people, the ones where everything came easy and the rest who worked hard. He had everything come to him easily, he was hard working and he was prosperous in life. At the time, I was unable to see my potential and experienced deep pain. For a few years into our marriage, I felt I was not worthy of having him as my husband. Over the past 14 years he has seen me change and has embraced the new me. He has given me unconditional love and encouraged me to evolve, I now believe that I am worthy and deserving of his love.

As a mother of two brilliant children— my daughter who is an over-achiever often refusing to believe in her abilities and strength, and my son, who has the challenge of learning. Modelling potential has been key in their success. Our children are a direct mirror image of who we are, I knew it was essential that I show how I "expressed possibilities." As they watched me attend each training, I did it with ease and belief that it was easy. They watched my business flourish while I worked with clients, developed training programs and designed and wrote a children's guided mediation. Modelling my belief of possibilities impacted how they see the world around them. They have adapted to the belief they are limitless in potential. My kids profoundly believe they can!

As I have transformed and created change, I realize I am on a journey. There is no perfect journey— only acceptance, surrender and belief that I am limitless in potential. I choose to see surrender as freedom to accomplish what I am meant to achieve on this planet. I now live my potential by expressing possibilities— I am an advocate, a leader, an entrepreneur, a wife, a daughter, a sister, a friend and a colleague. I am who I decide to be.

Making a limiting decision good or bad stems from experiences we have encountered. It can be a vague memory or an event that happens big or small— something that possibly is far beyond what we can recall. And yet, we make a decision at the unconscious level. The key is to make it your decision that you are limitless in your potential and begin the story of what you will be. Like any story, the best place to start is right at the beginning.

Teresa Scaini began her journey legacy a few years back, when she hit a major bump in the road. She found herself stuck and in pain struggling to find a solution. Part of the journey was discovering the power of the Unconscious Mind, that it was the gateway to all learning and change. Her story of pain has now unleashed the leader within her to empower and educate others.

Sarah Shakespeare

Running On All Engines– The 3 D's

Dedicated, Determined and Disciplined

So what does dedication, determination and discipline mean to me? It's a question that I have asked myself throughout my entire life. Are these words just too close to the words, obsessed, selfish and strict? I have been focused and ambitious from a very young age, as I have always wanted to accomplish many things in my life. I was drawn to energetic activities and strived to perform at my very best.

In my teenage years, I became interested in sports. It wasn't before long, that I realized, that running was my passion. As a teenager and especially as a mixed race teenager of Jamaican and English parents, the pressure was on to be a good runner. Jamaican sprinters were already ruling the track on the international circuit, so why couldn't I on the high school and district track?

With much focus and determination, I made it my mission to win every race that I ran. I practiced sprinting, watched races and visualized myself winning. I received much praise from my parents, especially my Jamaican father! My teachers, friends and family we extremely excited when I won my 100 meter sprints, which had become my favorite race. Now, if you are familiar with athletics, then you will know that the fastest runner always goes on the last leg of the 4x4 100m Relay. Therefore, my place was always on the 4th leg, and my responsibility was to bring it home for the team.

Throughout the four years of high school, I won every race that I had entered. I did not feel an external pressure from anyone. I just felt an internal drive, and of course at that age, I did not realize the gift that I had been given. I never knew how that gift of inner drive, discipline and determination would help me through some of the most intense times of my life.

Although a great athlete, I still carried extra weight that I can only blame on my mother's good home cooking! However, there was never any pressure to lose weight from anyone in my family.

At the age of 15, I decided to lose the extra weight that bothered me. I joined a weight loss group and lost 30 pounds. I was determined to lose the weight, and knew that the best time to get my body in order was when was young. I wanted a life that was full of vitality and energy. I had read so much about healthy eating and exercise and found it interesting. I knew that this would become an important part of my life.

I continued with a healthy eating regime and developed a joy of exercise outside of Track and Field. Group exercise classes became my new thing to love, and I joined a gym and discovered weight training. Now, back in the early 1990's, weight training wasn't something that young women did. You were expected to stay with good old fashioned aerobic classes.

I had my first child at the age of 18, and gained 65 pounds during that pregnancy. I knew that good nutrition, clean eating and exercise was the only way to lose the weight. I planned my meals ahead of time and exercised 6 days a week. I was serious about being an energetic young mother so, within the year, I had lost my weight and gone back to my pre-baby body. I was energized, happy and confident.

Throughout that year, many people questioned my dedication to my nutrition and exercise plan and called it an "obsession." When I look back at that time, there was no such thing as preparing food ahead of time. No one was eating out of plastic boxes that were taken from the fridge every few hours, or traveling with a cool box full of chicken and water bottles. I was extremely motivated and it showed! My weight was maintaining well and I started to look fit and healthy, and I liked it. I could play with my daughter for hours and had the energy to do so. I was so enthusiastic about my new lifestyle, that I would talk to many people about my results and the amazing benefits of exercise.

This is where the words, dedication, determination and discipline would start to be compared with the words of obsessed, selfish and strict by others. How would I start to deal with this? I felt successful, energetic and extremely pleased with myself that I had won again— this time at the weight loss game. I had not only lost weight during 12th grade, which is one of the busiest years at school, I had now lost 45 pounds of my baby weight.

Then an opportunity came knocking that I said yes to, without a hesitation! The owner of my gym had noticed my dedication, my weight loss triumph and my interaction with gym members.

I have always been a people person and it showed. I felt as though I was right at home in the gym environment and was interested in talking to fellow members about their fitness journeys. The owner offered to pay for my training to become a Personal Trainer and would give me a full-time job upon its completion. This was an amazing opportunity and I took it. I loved every minute of my classes and even loved reading the literature that others found boring. Was I really going to get paid for doing something that I loved doing everyday? Yes, I was about to embark on a career that didn't even feel like a job!

I loved my job and went on to also qualify as an Aerobic Instructor. Now I could dance around in a studio at work to loud music! I was so motivated to help people succeed with their fitness goals, and strived to be dedicated to each and every one of my clients. I even helped them make life decisions that they hadn't even shared with family and close friends. I became more than their Trainer and I liked it. I knew that my discipline to walk my talk and practice what I preach would go a long way with my clients.

I could empathize as I gone through the things that they were going through in my own life— whether it was lack of support from family and friends or the temptation of going back to foods that were now off the "plan." I had such joy and satisfaction that at the end of my working week, I knew that I had made a great impact in peoples lives.

My own workouts didn't suffer because I loved the gym and the aerobic studio. I didn't mind coming in early to start my workouts before work, and didn't mind staying on after work. I knew that you had to put the hours in to have optimum fitness. That may have meant sometimes doing my food prep at 1:00 a.m. before heading to work at 6:00 a.m. after a few short hours of sleep. I did whatever I needed to do, to stay focused and dedicated.

Although I loved the gym and group classes, I still craved to be outside running. I ran occasionally outside and then ended back inside on a treadmill. It was easier to get off the treadmill and pick up some dumbbells on a rack nearby, than it was to get changed and get outside pounding the pavement. It also didn't rain inside and since I lived in England at that time, the weather was always unpredictable. I knew deep down, that at some point, I would have to take up my passion for running again, and lose the excuse of worrying whether I would get caught in the rain!

The day came for me to take my running seriously again, and I decided to register for a half marathon.

My training changed from that point. It consisted of more outdoor running and less gym hours. However, even when I was caught in the rain I was happy to be back outside. Race day came and here I was with wearing a race number and feeling competitive. However, this time, there were hundreds of people in the race but I wasn't there to win it. I was there to finish it. My training hours on the road had been done and now. It was time to see if my feet would take me that far, comfortably. Well, they did! I secretly loved running past people who had been my targets ahead of me, a few minutes before. It felt good and I was completely in my element. I ran a couple more half marathons after that race, before I decided to try a full marathon.

This time, I knew that I had to be very strong to complete a 26-mile circuit. My weight training had played a big part of my training— and many long runs would be put into my already busy schedule. My focus and inner drive made sure that I didn't miss a session. I was excited to get my race number on again and wanted to see how my body would feel over these 26 miles.

Many questions entered my head. Would I be tired? Would I pull a muscle? Would it rain? It was a more focused group at the starting line. I was excited! It felt like we were on official business. I suppose we all knew that— all of the many hours of training had to count for something.

The race was long and the weather was good. It was an amazing feeling to go past the turnoff sign that said "Half Marathon this way" as I continued to run ahead. It meant that I had to now do my original race all over again in one day! Could I do it? How did I feel? Yes, I could do it because I had put in the training hours. I was feeling a little tired, but amazed that I felt energetic enough to keep on going.

As I finished the race, it felt like I was crossing the line at the Olympics when I heard the MC mention my name as I crossed the finish line. I was given a medal and my first marathon was done. I am very goal-orientated, so it was another goal checked off the list.

My legs started to feel heavy as I walked to the car and that is when I realized that yes, my body had just taken me around a 26-mile course. My body would ache until Wednesday, so there was no chance of me committing to another marathon anytime soon, especially when I could not even sit down comfortably!

As the days passed, I started to realize just how well my body had performed and I was recovering well. So, it was time to look into more races and start to take this new love for running seriously again. My next marathon went well and I was hooked on the running game. I felt strong and fit. I was pleased that now, during my 20's, my passion for running was back and that my gym training helped so much in my performance. I was happy as I was reaching more of my fitness goals. Although I loved running outside again and had made many wonderful friends through the sport, I still had an absolute passion for weight training. I loved the strength and fitness level that it gave me.

I was busy teaching aerobic classes and enjoyed the interaction with the participants. It was then, that I started to take an interest in fitness competitions. It wasn't the masculine body-building side that I was intrigued about, it was these amazingly fit women that were on stage. They were feminine, beautiful, fit and strong. I began to watch a few competitions and to say that it sparked an interest in me, is an understatement. You had to wear a bikini, sportswear, evening gown and do a 2-minute dance routine.

A few weeks later, a show was coming to my town and I thought that I would watch it and just see what it entailed. During the week before the show many people at my gym asked me if I was going to be in the Fitness Show that was coming up at the weekend. I happily said "No, I'm just watching, I don't do shows, I am a marathon runner."

The day of the show arrived and I was excited to go and see what this was all about. I arrived at the venue and approached the box office to purchase my ticket. The member of the staff said, "All competitors go through that door over there, you don't need a ticket." I answered back by saying "I am not in the show. I have come to watch." "You're not in the show?" he quickly answered. "You look like you should be in the show." He went on to tell me registration was still open and that if I was interested, I could register right there and then. I asked what I needed, and was told, bikini, sportswear, dress and a 2-minute dance routine. I already knew that, since I had been watching the shows for a while now on television.

So in that minute, I made the decision to enter the show! It would be my first show, and I didn't even feel nervous about that decision. I drove home, picked up what I needed and then went back to the venue and this time went through the "Competitors Door." I was greeted by fit, enthusiastic girls who had trained hard for the event. It was amazing to be amongst ladies who went to the gym everyday and sometimes twice a day! I was completely in my element. I felt as though my dedication, discipline and determination throughout my fitness journey had put me in the right room at last. I was somewhere where I was not going to be called obsessed, selfish or strict and I liked it!

I have a "natural suntan" as I am mixed race, so I didn't need a spray tan. I already looked "competition ready."

I went out on stage and did exactly what I had seen in the competitions that I had watched on television. I could walk well in high heels because I wore heels everyday when I wasn't in gym clothing. I had taught aerobics for 12-years so, I put together a 2-minute routine on the spot. I felt as though the show went well and I was confident on stage. Then the announcement came... I had won the show! Had I really won a show that I hadn't trained for? Yes, I had! I had that amazing feeling back that I had back in high school when I used to win all of my races. My win qualified me for the finals that were to be held in 6 weeks. I was already training a lot so, I worked towards the finals. I ended up winning that competition too!

I was still running and entering marathons and pushing my body to its limits. That's when someone at my running club said "have you thought about ultra marathons?" Was I ready to run 2 marathons in one day? It would take some hard training but I had that inner drive to succeed. I trained with amazing people and worked towards my first 'ultra marathon.' This had me training on some days, for 5 hours a day. Luckily, I wasn't working at this time, as I was at home with my children. Therefore, I could dedicate many hours to my training. I did my first 50km, and although it was on rough terrain, and it was steep and long, I truly felt proud when I finished the race. I then registered for a 50-mile race that was coming up in next few months.

My interest in competitions had not gone away, so I looked into what it would take to get on a bigger stage with a larger fitness federation. I wanted to get my Pro Card on the fitness stage and promised myself that I would work as hard as I could to achieve that goal.

So I entered my first competition with a big federation. I knew that the caliber of athletes would be high, and this may not be an easy win for me. However, I trained hard and hired a choreographer who put together an amazing routine for me. There was no making up a routine on the spot this time! Your points gained on stage were for your complete package. This meant that your routine had to be a "show stopper" to gain attention. This was the road that I had to take to get a Pro Card.

The weekend of the competitions approached and I was ready and focused. I was excited to get on stage as I had many family and friends in the audience this time. My routine had been practiced many times a day, my nutrition had been good and I had been able to run well during my competition training.

I loved being on the bigger stage and felt at home up there. For me to achieve, reach the finals, and qualify to be in The World Championships, I had to get into the Top 3. Pro Cards were only given to the winners at the Championships. I absolutely had to get on that Championship Stage to even have a chance of a getting a Pro Card. My routine was executed perfectly and my posing and evening gown round went well.

The announcements came in. I came in 2nd, which meant I could go to The World Championships and try for my Pro Card. It was the most amazing feeling, and although I hadn't won, I had qualified to get on the stage that I really wanted to be on. The Championships were in 6 weeks.

I was registered for both the ultra marathon and a marathon that year, so I kept up my running training as well as my competition training. When I checked my upcoming events it became apparent that I had a competition on one weekend and a full marathon the next. Was my body really up for that? My mental strength as well as my physical strength were definitely being put to the test. I committed to doing both events a week apart from each other. I started 6 weeks of intense training and it felt like it was my full-time job.

My goal was to qualify for the Boston Marathon so I knew that I would have to run my fastest marathon to date to even get a qualifying time. My 2 goals in that month were to get a Pro card and qualify to run the Boston Marathon. I knew that they were huge goals, but it seemed that the timing was perfect.

I did not miss a day of scheduled training, I knew that for every day I had off there was a competitor against me who had not had a day off.

I was excited and ready to get on stage. I arrived the registration of the show and everyone there looked extremely fit. Was I nervous? Not really. I had been doing this for a long time and was ready to take it to the next level. I spent the day at the hotel relaxing, as I focused on what I had to do the next day on stage. I didn't do anything that took an ounce of energy out of me. I listened to my dance routine music so that I could go through the moves in my mind.

It was the day of the Championships and I was rested, relaxed and ready to go. I called my father on the way to the competition to chat with him about the day ahead. He said "Keep your eye on the ball darling, this is your Olympics. You have been training for this day for years, but you didn't know it. You can win this competition." He was right, I had been training hard for years and not really knowing what was going to come from it. I loved being fit of course, but he was right, this was my Olympics!

Backstage at the show was electrifying. I was in the company of some incredible athletes who took their fitness and health as seriously as I did. They too, were motivated and there to win.

My name and number were called and I was ready to go! It was time for me to showcase all of my hard work. So I did just that— I felt energized and happy to be on stage and performed everything, including my routine to the best of my ability. I left the stage feeling fulfilled, knowing that I could not have done a single thing better.

It was a long day and the announcements were not until that evening. Then at 9:00 p.m., it was time for me to get back on stage for the placing announcements. They called out the Top 10 and I heard my name! Excellent news, as the standard of athletes on stage was amazing. I felt privileged to have made the Top 10. Then they called the Top 5 and yes my name was called again. Wow! It was the most amazing feeling. I stood alongside some of the most conditioned athletes and I felt honored to be there! Then came the announcement of the Top 3 and my name was called again, was I getting closer to a Pro Card? I was excited and nervous at the same time. I kept thinking about my dad saying "This is your Olympics, and you can win."

The excitement in the crowd and on the stage was at an all time high and then they announced the Top 2 girls. I was in the Top 2 and in-line for a Pro Card. Many athletes try for many years to get a Pro Card and many times do not succeed. I thought, "ok, so if today wasn't my day then I could go again." I then heard the Head Judge say my name, yes my name!! The excitement had me jumping up and down in my high heels because I had just got my Pro Card on my first attempt! This was an incredible feeling and one of my proudest moments.

I left the stage and my first phone call was to my father who was waiting at home by the phone for the results. I said "Dad I got the ball, I kept my eye on the ball and I won!" He said "I knew you would darling, because this was your Olympics."

I left the show with a heavy glass trophy but my biggest reward was that I could now compete in the Pro Division as I was a Pro Athlete. My hard work and focus and yes, maybe this time, I had been obsessed, selfish and extremely strict, but I was on a mission to win and I did just that!

Now I had to get home and replenish my body as I had a marathon to run next week. I had to qualify for the Boston Marathon, which is an elite marathon— that only fastest, pre-qualified runners can take part in.

Race day arrived. I had my number pinned on my shirt and was ready to go! I focused on the time and planned out my speed so that I could come in at the required time. It was a sunny day with no rain in the forecast, so nothing should hold me back. I pushed every mile and watched the clock closely. I was on track for my qualifying time. I was going to do this if I concentrated and kept my speed up. I came in at my desired time and qualified for the Boston Marathon. What a week it had been for me! Now it was time for a rest!

I looked at the date of the upcoming Boston Marathon and it was around the same time as the 50-mile ultra. I was keen to do the ultra, as I had already put in many hours in training for it. So, I made the decision to go ahead and do the ultra instead. I commended myself for running 2 marathons in one day. I then registered for my biggest race that I would run as an Ultra Runner, a 100km race that was coming up at the end of the year. Competitions hadn't disappeared off the radar— I had my Pro Card, so at some point, I would stand on a Pro Athlete Stage.

I soon heard that there was a Pro Show in Miami. It was somewhere that I had wanted to visit my entire life. I decided to enter, trained hard for it and flew to the show. When I arrived at the show registration, I was excited to see that my photograph was on the poster advertising the show!

The competition was difficult, and given that it was my first Pro Show, I was excited to come in 5th. To get into the Top 5 for me, was amazing, and a good way to step out of doing competitions. My goal of receiving a Pro Card had been met, so it was time to get on with other goals in my life.

To date I have done 5 half marathons, 12 marathons and 3 ultra marathons. I continue to run and and weight train and still love it as much as when I started many years ago. When I look back on my years of competing at a high level and think about how I pushed my body to the max, what did it teach me?

It has taught me that you must always have a goal in life that suits you and that you must never lose sight of that goal. When you are helping others to goal set and excel in their lives, you can only truly help them if you are motivated yourself. It's so important to have an action plan and work towards following that. Get ready for obstacles in life that will hold you back. Plan ahead so that you are equipped with the tools and support systems to get through those obstacles. It is also important to have patience and realize that things do not happen overnight.

Having that inner drive and ambition on the athletic side of my life has helped me in the real side of my life as well. It has made me want to personally excel and help others to excel too. Being dedicated, determined and disciplined makes me who I am. THAT'S WHY I AM BORN TO BE ME!

Sarah Shakespeare has always lived her with a "Glass is Full" attitude. As a Personal Trainer and Coach for nearly 25 years she loves to help people enrich their life through creating a healthy lifestyle. As someone who is very goal driven, she has come to know that success really comes from first sculpting a positive mindset. She is a wife, mother of three daughters was born and raised in England. She lives in beautiful British Columbia, Canada and feels lucky everyday to live in her dream destination!

Carol Starr Taylor

I'm too ~~Sexy~~ Fat for...
Body Image, Self-Esteem and Self-Worth

Social media is inundated with positive affirmations on how we should love ourselves and everyone around us. We are taught tolerance and yet experience bullying in different forms through what I like to coin "silent bullying— ageism, fatism (as I call it) and different ways on how we view ourselves and how others see us.

Even though we may have a strong personality and positive sense of self, we all look in the mirror, both men and women, and we nitpick at all our own flaws. A big one for men is looking at their thinning hair, so the style of the shaved head has become common place.

We look at our crows feet, double chin, laugh lines, boobs— too big or too small— our thighs, butts, and everything in between. Parts of our bodies have become our nemesis. In the age of #firstworldproblems, even fit individuals look at themselves with some distain, silently criticizing themselves on how to look and feel better.

We can't help getting older, of course, but it is how we handle it. Self-confidence is sexy. Being confident doesn't discount that we all have our secret insecurities that eat us up. It is really how we carry ourselves and dress for our age and body type regardless of how old we are.

In this case men and women are alike.

Do your insecurities stop you from doing the things you want to do because of a secret fear of how others will view you?

Do you not date the person you want because you think they are "out of your league"?

Do you not date because you think that others won't find you attractive or sexy?

Do you fear rejection?

Do you stop doing physical activities or extreme adventures for fear of how you look?

Do you take pictures of others and hate pictures of yourself so you aren't in any?

Do you not go on vacation for fear of going out in a bathing suit?

Do you not go to certain resorts because "everyone there" has perfect bodies?

Do you crop your pictures to only show your face? We have ALL been culprits of this.

Are you self-conscious when you engage in sexual relations for fear of what your body looks and feels like? Are you thinking that your body doesn't measure up, and all of those "parts" aren't the way they use to look, feel and move? Are you focused on your body parts as gravity has hit and things aren't all in the same place anymore? Have you put on weight and now there is a jiggle, where jiggle shouldn't be? Are you not enjoying sex in the way you should be, because of your thoughts interfering?

Personally, one of the reasons I dislike flying (although It has never stopped me) is that those seats are getting smaller and my butt just doesn't want to fit so neatly without some "spillage." I have felt embarrassed in the past, mortified that the seat belt might actually not fit so perfectly across my body.

Thankfully, I have grown to embrace and accept that I am perfectly imperfect. This is a work in progress for me. Am I always going to be like this? I truly believe no, but I realize that this is the ME of NOW. Acceptance.

Think about what you stop doing or do not do because of how you look and feel?

How others view you is never worse than how you view yourself. We constantly beat ourselves up with Self-Talk.

I know that I'm not alone in this. I am my worst enemy in the age of fatism.

An example of this is when I decide to "treat" myself to my favorite frappuccino or ice cream/gelato. I think when I am consuming it everyone is looking at me thinking "no wonder she's fat, look at what she's drinking or eating." Are people actually thinking this? Some may be... but most people couldn't care less. Why should we really even care? These people are total strangers. But we do care. Our own fatism insecurities are taking our whole enjoyment out of the "treat."

"I've talked to so many people, men and women alike, that get overweight and their self-esteem just goes in the tank. They think they're judged. They think they're unattractive."
~ Phil McGraw

Like most people who have struggled with their weight - my closet is filled with clothes I can wear, clothes I used to wear, and clothes I hope to wear when I lose the weight.

Do you think that only women are the ones struggling with negative self-talk? Think again.

There is a constant bombardment of pictures of men on social media with washboard six packs, full kissable lips, hairless bodies drinking a cup of Joe, or firefighters with no shirts. Women are sending these messages to guys out there, see guys that's what WE like. We want you like that! Men joking that they have the "24 pack" the beer belly, the two pack, and the list goes on. Those images also put men in the same downward spiral of self-loathing that we all know and have experienced. Men experience the same negative emotions as females do. They just do not express the same way women do. They stay all stoic and "man up." Men have many insecurities that they do not always express ranging from hair loss, gynecomastia (man boobs), penis size, their height, erectile dysfunction (ED), and measuring up in the bedroom just to name a few. Most of these issues, men have no control over and can't change them through lotions, potions, and exercise.

Have I ever been the recipient of the silent bullying from fatism and ageism? One hundred percent yes. Although I do not look my age, there is no hiding the fact that A) I am no longer in my 20's and 30's and B) that I am overweight. Do I look like a reality show contestant that can't get out of bed? No. But, I have not gotten jobs because I'm too old and not gotten promotions or work opportunities in certain industries because I do not "look the part." So what did I do? I became self employed. I am driven and realize that I refuse to be defined by my age or physical appearance but by my abilities, outward confident persona, and confidence.

My motto is that "fear will not stop me from doing what I want to do." I know that self employment is not an option for everyone. That is how I have personally dealt with it. Thinking outside the box is how warriors will overcome the obstacles they face.

Although I am not an expert in health and fitness, I am an expert in the yo-yo diet. I have pictures in different stages of weight gain and weight loss. However, I will not allow myself to be defined by my weight. But hold on... am I actually being judged by the outside world or is it Me doing it to myself?

Can any of you relate?

The myth in society is that if you are fat, you have no control. NOT TRUE. Let's face it... shit happens in life. You can't go through life without any chaos. There are posts saying that "you never know what battles people are fighting." Right, you do not! We are told not to judge others and show love to everyone around you.

We all age differently, and yes, many of us have to also keep fighting the weight battle because we are in the mode of controlling other aspects of our lives. Many of us have experienced feelings of despair due to losing a loved one, money, relationship, health issues, and other stressors that have consumed us at one time or another. At these times, we sometimes "let ourselves go." Divorce, family, children, work, health and monetary issues, for example, certainly take their toll on us. It is how we react, how resourceful we are, and how quickly we recover from these factors that determine our successful outcome. That is character! That is control! That is positive self-talk. The outcome of overcoming these major life challenges is that we neglect the one person we shouldn't: ourselves.

Oh yes, like everyone, I have pictures of myself in my 20's when my daily diet consisted of huge doses of coffee, cigarettes, aerobics classes, nautilus machines, sex, and dancing at clubs with friends both Friday and Saturday nights. And, oh boy, did I look hot! Carefree and living the life as I knew it.

Then of course when you start working full-time and the spread begins, so onto the frantic yo-yo dieting to get my body in bridal perfect shape. Done! Well, bridal perfect didn't last too long after the wedding.

So as I am growing up into a married lady, cooking for two, my husband and I, working full-time, the challenges of a newlywed, including the financial struggles of being a young and hopeful couple, there doesn't seem time to do any of those things that helped me maintain my perfect early 20's body. (I battled it in childhood and my teens but in my early 20's seemed to have conquered it or so I thought).

In the years of 30's and mid 40's were totally consumed with having children, working, family and the long drives in the car to and from the children's sports activities, not only did my metabolism abandon me - I ABANDONED ME!

My yo-yo dieting during that time didn't help. Finally, after losing quite a bit of weight and achieving a new found confidence in my early 40's, I felt I could conquer the world!

By my mid-40's, I was separated from a long-term marriage and found myself with a fresh exuberance and a sense of freedom with this curvy thin(ish) body ready to "get out there" to see what I have missed.

The euphoria of singledom wore off to the reality of going through a divorce, bills, lawyer bills, and trying to find a job with battling the silent ageism bully as each prospective employer shut the door in my face. In addition to being unemployable, (I was told by some off the record, of course, because of my age and experience), my weight skyrocketed. With each passing year the yo-yo was in full swing doing loop de loops— not in my favor.

Aging, slower metabolism, stress— we all at one time or another have or will experience it.

For weight loss, experts tell us to choose a picture from our past. Post it on the fridge or keep it in our wallet for motivation. Does this work for you? It doesn't for me. Why? Pictures illicit emotion. Good or bad. Yes, it is a snapshot showing your former self. That in a nutshell is exactly why it doesn't work for me. Yes, I look gorgeous and "skinny" in that picture. But that person in the picture no longer exists— mind, body, or soul. That person is a stranger with different hopes and dreams, goals, different experiences, stressors, and a different outlook of life. That person is part of the journey but not the end of it. It is me in the picture, but not the ME of now. To continue to journey, is to create a new normal. Identify and visualize the new me, the me that is comfortable in my own skin, understanding that I am not perfect and I am not in competition with anyone other than myself. Create a realistic goal, a sustainable one. The goal should be one that fits into the person I am today, work toward success how I have defined it, and no one else.

I can say that through the journey, lots of life lessons have been learned. Life occurs in pieces. There will be many more to come. What has emerged from all of this is a more self-confident, self-aware person. Yes, I play these games with my secret self. I am human. And so are you. As I do, be grateful and count your blessings, and also be proud of your accomplishments.

Sometimes the little self doubt voice creeps into my head. The difference is that instead of beating myself up I try to turn it around. Self-talk with positivity.

Just when we think we have it all figured out, our fatism whisperer comes calling. STOP listening.

I will give you an example of an experience I had. Here I am, on a healthier path, mind, body, and soul. Professionally, totally thrilled that I secured this amazing video interview for an entertainment vlog I was writing and producing, with an up-and-coming star and fairly well known in many circles— so proud of myself, of course, for the coup. Loving myself and all I have achieved. Being on film, as my outward persona is flying high, and, at the same time, my insecurities come flooding back, thinking I look terrible on camera, I'm too fat to interview on tape, I have a body for radio, and I am totally sure that the entertainer's mother is younger than me to boot.

Wow, why did I do that to myself?! Just when things are looking up, I can be my own saboteur. I quickly put it into perspective. Oprah, as we have witnessed, has battled her weight in front of the whole world. She's on camera! So why is little old me beating myself up about it being fat on camera? I should learn from Oprah! She is a Goddess. She is OPRAH! Many entertainers put themselves out there and we have seen their weight loss and weight gain struggle before our very eyes. Does it take away from their talent? Of course not! Their beauty? No. What it shows me is bravery, character, and kick-ass gumption.

I will not be defined by my weight nor will I let anything or anyone stop me. FEAR IS A KILLER OF DREAMS. I know it sounds cliché, but clichés are born because we all experience this. You and I are not alone.

You and I are not so different. Young, old, fat, thin, fit, or not fit— we all experience similar emotions. We all have demons we face. We all have moments where we think "coulda, woulda, shoulda." It is normal to do so... just as I have learned not wallow in it.

I truly believe that attitude is everything. I never consider anything a "failure." It is another way to re-adjust and look at things from a different perspective to see how I can move forward: how many times I can get up and how resilient I can be.

We are all on our own personal journeys. Do not be a "victim" of ageism or fatism, especially from your own self. STOP focusing on what is wrong with yourself and look more into what is right. We all need to make changes in some form or another. That is called personal growth. Realize that you are a work in progress. Always look ahead, move forward, and never look back because we do not want to go there.

Why is it so difficult for many of us to accept a compliment? Do you have difficulty with receiving? The answer to working with this issue is self-talk. We often belittle the compliment in our minds. Oh, they didn't really mean it. Oh, they said I look great. Do I? Yes, maybe my hair, but I look tired. I'm still fat. WHY? WHY DO WE DO THIS TO OURSELVES? Why is it so difficult to believe and accept love?

I knew a woman, who at the time was close to death. She actually didn't realize that she was loved. Yes, that is sad. If you do not think the love and compliments are coming from an authentic place, then I would suggest to associate with people that ARE AUTHENTIC! Over the years, I have learned to accept the compliment as sincere. It has been challenging, after years of negative self talk, but I did conquer that, for the most part. Do I still catch myself with negative self talk? Yes, of course, at times. I try to catch myself in mid thought.

YOU MUST BELIEVE THAT YOU ARE WORTHY, BEAUTIFUL, LOVED, AND YES, ABOVE ALL YOU ARE ENOUGH. Say this to yourself, all the time, every day. I AM BEAUTIFUL INSIDE AND OUT, I AM LOVED, AND I AM ENOUGH. When you start to believe this, embrace it, you not only will be able to accept the compliment, you will revel in it!

Carol Starr Taylor is the Founder of Creative Publishing Group, Writing Coach, Certified Life Coach, NLP Practitioner, International Bestselling Author of the book Life In Pieces—From Chaos to Clarity, Inspirational Speaker, Soulprenuer, and the Founder of The Travelling Sisterhood.
She has appeared on TV, Radio, and has been featured in numerous articles. Her passion is to inspire and help facilitate the personal growth of others within themselves and with each other.

Denise K. Venuto

The House That Built Me

When I was little, I remember my Mom cutting out pictures of houses from Better Homes and Garden Magazine for years. Plans were drawn and concrete poured. Nail by nail and board by board, my Dad gave life to Mom's dreams. They were successful at building homes for themselves and others. In the process of home building however, they forgot to build the very solid foundation in their own home, with love, laughter and peace. They worked hard and reaped the financial rewards, and I admired them for that. My three sisters and myself, were always taken care of in material ways.

However, as far as family closeness, bonding and ensuring we were tight as a unit, not so much. There had been animosity, anger and sadness on Mom's part, for one reason or another. Was she stressed? 4 kids and a business to maintain. That could send any one off into the deep end. I know too well the effects of anxiety and depression having my own business and 2 kids. Being self-employed, has its advantages, but trying to be the perfect daughter, wife, mother, it clearly has its down sides. Never-ending hours, always on call, handling most of the situations yourself, the administration, the employees, the decisions, the bills, the kids, the family, the house, cooking, cleaning. It can consume you. Chew you up and spit you out. Passionate, driven, family oriented women, sacrifice a lot of themselves for the sake of everyone else. So where is the breaking point?

At a very young age you would find me in the garden, looking at plants, picking and eating cherries, playing with the animals, staring or collecting bugs. Anything animal, critters and outdoors, I was all over it. Pictures of me with two cats hanging off my arms. More like me having them in a choke hold comes to my mind. I just wanted to love them, cuddle them, squeeze them, and take care of them. Chasing chickens, dressed in suspender jean pants and a handkerchief around my neck, in my grand-mother's yard, is where you would find me. I was at peace when I was outdoors. A cute, dark, curly haired little cherub, I was. Pretty much a happy kid, until we moved from our city home to our home in the suburbs.

My father, was a fair skinned, blue-eyed, young, handsome, Italian immigrant. Hardworking by nature, simple by lifestyle, a man with big dreams. He did all he could to make Mom happy, or at least what he thought brought her happiness, which ultimately wasn't all house building. My Mom was looking for more, I think. Only now can I sit back and reflect and understand her better. Being that I too, am a driven, hardworking, passionate, woman myself. They sacrificed so much in attaining their dreams to the cost and detriment of family relationships.

Happiness was not at the forefront of life in our home. It was about breaking concrete and putting up wooden frames, constructing homes, which resulted in our own shaky foundation.

As a child, like any child, I looked up to both of my parents. I remember my Dad coming home after a long, hard, hot, day of construction work, full of sawdust in his hair, shirtless and tanned. I would just stare up at him, with eyes wide open, in awe. Thinking to myself, I was going to marry someone like that one day. My Super Hero! He would scoop me up in his arms with a big smile, asking me how my day was, putting me on his motorcycle and taking me for a spin around the yard. Very few of those memories, I hold onto them like thieves in the night.

Can you imagine 4 kids, 3 of which were all under the age of 3.5 years old by the age of 22, with the last one, arriving by the time you were 25? They bit off more than they could chew. Actually, I do remember, how upset my grandparents were finding out that my Mom was pregnant with the last one. I myself was not happy about adding another child into this craziness. Already, at 7 years old I had seen and been through enough to realize my Mom and Dad couldn't handle all us kids, plus every-thing else. But they were determined to try for that boy. Sadly, for them, that never happened, finally making peace with that after my 4th sister was born.

My Mom, a dark haired, Italian beauty, with a smile that could light up a room, when she did smile. She was a wiry, energetic type, always on edge and moody, always bickering with some-one or about someone. Just a real heavy, argumentative type, bossy and controlling, a ticking time bomb. I remember thinking to myself why can't she just loosen up and be happy? I think I know now why she liked her wine. Nonetheless, I looked up to her, thinking she was the most beautiful thing.

With four girls, a growing construction business, a house in the suburbs, a dog and grandparents close enough to help out once in a while, you would have thought life would be good. But sadly, our story is not like the one of 'Little Women.'

I see my parents in the kitchen, at the table— square, dark brown with natural wood striations and large enough to sit all 6 of us. My parents started planning, my Dad's determination and my Mom's dreams push forward. They planned their business and ideas, always believing they were doing it for the best of the family. Somewhere along the way things went haywire.

That table... the arguments always started between them at that kitchen table. It then escalated to yelling matches to which my grandparents were also on the receiving end. I felt sad, confused, and worried. Mom would antagonize Dad and of course, he was becoming ever more, nervous and agitated. But they persevered and so did I. Then one day I saw the worst of it when Dad hit Mom or was it Mom hit Dad? The craziness ensued and I lost my innocence.

The house that built me also broke me.

I had to deal with some pretty heavy things and heard some pretty ugly things. My mother who had amazing command of the English language, used her tongue well. She would ridicule and name call, him and us. My father would lose it and they were often at each other's throats. Plates, glasses, bedrooms smashed to pieces, right in front of our very eyes. My poor sisters. The looks on their faces. Heartbreaking. It was terrifying.

I would typically stand up for my Dad which only made matters worse. I would see the hurt in his eyes from the ugliness of the words my Mom would use on him. She would make fun of his accent, his poor English, reading and writing skills. I hurt for my Dad and I started to speak up, but that was not a good move on my part. I guess I learned defiance at a young age which, in one way was a saving grace, on the other not so much. My Mom began to resent me and I her, our relationship started to deteriorate.

At some point I started to think that they actually enjoyed this behavior. It did not seem like it ever, truly bothered them. The day after, life went on as usual, business went on as usual. The dust settled and everyone pretended as if nothing happened. Everything was back to "normal." But there was no normal in the house that built me.

I always lived on constant high alert, in either fight or flight mode. I felt I was always to blame. Such a heavy load for a child and young person to bear. Being the oldest, I also felt an obligation to my younger sisters to protect them from the worst of it, so I took it all on, as much as I could, ushering them into hiding places, telling them to plug their ears and close their eyes. I would often physically place myself between the two of them to get them to stop. Crying, and screaming at them to stop.

It made me tough, resilient and a fighter but for the good cause! I transcended during these episodes. Putting my life and well-being aside for them. To get them to see, to hear, to feel. They never saw me, heard me or felt me. Getting through school was tough, but through life, a miracle. To focus and study through the chaos, that would ensue, every 3 months, like clockwork, was gruelling to say the least. I became an expert at keeping track and timing the blow outs. A perfect storm always brewing.

The physical abuse ended when I got too big but the verbal abuse started with a vengeance, both for myself and my sisters. When I got older, I would plan my escapes, to be away for days, weeks, even months at a time, traveling south or to Europe. Whenever I could just to get away. My life experiences, made me, grew me, and shaped me.

Amongst the thorns a rose did bud. I pushed through and preserved. As they say, 'what doesn't kill you only makes you stronger.' I knew it wasn't forever. I needed the dark to see the light. I had my secret hiding spot on the side of the house and there, I would convene with God. I truly don't know what I would have done without him. He guided me and told me, "you must learn to keep dying." So that is what I did. Every time something happened, I would die and come back. Not litersally, but metaphorically.

Hearts were hurt, minds were bruised, especially the kids. Nothing was ever done to try to mend that. Nothing. It seemed that houses were always more important and this behavior affected all of us.

At some point, I had lost respect for both of them. Life in my younger adult years was how best to get through school without killing them or myself and get the hell out. I learned from the best — the good traits and bad ones. I was an exemplary student. Monkey see, monkey do. I grew up valuing hard work but at the cost of relationships. Like all children, they watch, they listen and they learn.

As I continued up the stairs of the house that built me, I was struck by flashbacks of me racing up and down the stairs in search of my sisters. I saw myself on my tippy-toes looking out of my bedroom window. In that little bedroom facing the backyard is where I did my homework and cried myself to sleep many nights. Wishing, hoping someone would come up and comfort me, tell me it was going to be alright. My favorite dog and I grew up in that backyard. Looking at it now, seems all so small.

That backyard... I see that peach tree there. My sisters and I planted that tree. I picked a peach off that tree and have never eaten a peach quite like that ever again. I still remember the fuzziness and how it felt on my lips and tongue, the sweet juice.

This house that built me, is very significant. It holds the best and worst memories. It made me, it broke me, and it made me again.

I thought if I could touch this place again, feel it, that somehow this brokenness inside me might start healing. I thought maybe I could find myself out there, but the more I drove away, the more the memories would not leave. If only I could come in and walk through the rooms one last time. I would leave with nothing but a memory, for the house that built me lives within me.

Over thinking has always been my thing. Fear has been my friend and feelings of inadequacy have robbed me of so many opportunities. These have lead me down the safe path, the comfort zone. Many of us feel more comfortable and safe being invisible, yet we also want to be seen, heard and felt.

I need to believe that there is a higher good, God, a truth, Universe, whatever you want to call it. It is here for humanities sake, it is here, for me. To frame my life, my work, who I am as an individual, here on earth. If you look at the grand scale of things, we, humans, have been evolving for the past 2,000 years, documented. Only 2,000 years, really isn't so long, in the 'big picture', and even bigger relative to Universe. It really is a "blink of an eye." I've laid the thought and foundation to thinking bigger which has helped me to believe that there must be a higher good, a God.

I'm a 43-year-old, woman, Mother. I have been here for a fraction of that "blink of an eye." Get where I am going with this? I don't know if I have tomorrow. I hope I do, as every day is a gift, but we really don't know. Today is a gift, tomorrow is unknown. As much as I'm a thinker, over-thinking doesn't produce results, so I'm set on proving myself through my actions.

"The mind is a wonderful servant, but a terrible master."
~Robin Sharma

My choices and decisions have been about following my heart, with some logical rationale, hard work and perseverance. I am where I am today because of what I have manifested for myself. No one helped me. Some would like to say they did, some would say they were the catalyst, some have robbed me of it. It has all been me, ultimately.

I truly believe we are all born to be ourselves, with a certain blueprint— which we forget, as soon as we are born. Add on top of that a lengthy list of rules, experiences (good and bad) and guidelines to live by, some very contradicting, influenced by familial, societal, cultural, religious beliefs. Living this human existence has been tough right from the onset. Add a pinch of this and a splash of that with a number of life changing events, it can sometimes make you feel lost, bewildered and confused. But believe me when I say that the amount of work that has been put into making me and you, is so damn worth it and the journey spectacular!

I was made to be distinctly someone, and so were you. On a number of different occasions, for different reasons, at different phases in my life, I had to stop and ask myself some tough questions. One of which was, what impact will I have on the world? Even on a small scale, in my own home, with my children, in my community. How can I be the best version of myself at all times? I would ask Universe, God, our higher good, even as a small child. I knew, the way I was growing up was not the way I wanted to live as an adult. That I did not want to bestow that kind of anguish and grief unto anyone else.

Firstly, I set myself to task. Finishing school was top priority to me. I knew that if I finished school I'd find work that would pay me well. I could buy my own home and move out. That is what I did. Secondly, I met a young man on my travels, we fell in love, got married and had children of our own. Thirdly, I decided that corporate life was no longer fulfilling me so I decided to leave and start my own business, while having two small children. With some gruelling sacrifices, hard work, tears, frustration, betrayal, loss, grief and disappointments, I am still standing.

I understand more and know more now, than my parents ever did. I have learned that balance is key. If something isn't working for you, then stop before it takes over, even ruins your life. The very relationships we are here to build and nurture, with those most important in our life, should not be sacrificed. Nothing is that important when we are living in a "blink of an eye", especially with our children.

I have chosen to set my mind on things above, not on things that are on earth or of this earth. For I died in that house and my life was brought back to me for the greater good.

It is not what happens to us, but what we do with it that defines us as human beings. Through writing this, I have come to abandon all the things that have happened to me that made me believe certain things about myself that aren't true, that have restricted me from being who I was born to be, completely and in my entirety. For each and every one of us, something happens that leads to a feeling, be it rejection, fear or elation or pride. That becomes a belief deeply ingrained and carefully coddled. In turn, that belief turns into the ways we choose to cope with things and live our lives. I want to grow, expand, rise above, soar, and in writing, this happens.

The house that built me is constantly being reframed. I do not build my dreams and life on houses, but on how I have shaped the people I meet and am close to in positive ways, as much as possible. Like a very good friend said to me:

"Everything we go through is preparing us to stop a flood,
or save a life, or make someone smile. It's so damn worth it."
~Leo E.

I am not perfect. I don't need to be, as I believe that God loves me the way I am, as he knows and sees that I am working on it. I am working on finding my way back home. I fall, but I rise again, and I will not be ruled by money or power, greed or position, but by light and love.

"Maybe the journey is not so much about becoming anything.
Maybe it is about un-becoming everything that is not really you,
so you can be who you were meant to be in the first place."
~Unknown

Denise K. Venuto, 13+ years in corporate business as a marketing and sales manager and consultant, with a proven system to get your business from negative to positive.

A certified Health Coach, Sustainable Local Food Advocate and a WISDOM Coach ™ she mentors kids, youth and families, making family wellness and mental health top priority.

She works with her clients on a project to project basis, setting achievable goals smoothly and successfully.

Heather Wilson

Guiding Principles for Discovering My Purpose

On May 3rd, 2006 my sister called me and said the words you never want to hear, "They took my children!" I was stunned and immediately asked, "What do you mean? Who took your children?!" "Children's Aid did. Someone said there was too much fighting, so CAS took them." She had been doing her best to raise her two children, but having a tough time. My parents and I helped whenever we could, but she lived 3 1/2 hours away, which made it difficult to be there for her and the kids.

My heart raced, as I tried to understand what was happening. I put on my best calm voice and asked, "Okay, where did they take them?"

"They're going to a foster home, I don't where, and they won't tell me." She replied.

"Okay, I am coming to see you. Let me see what day I can get off work. I am coming to see you, I promise, as soon as I can." I emailed my boss that night and was able to get May 8th off work.

The months following that, were filled with booking two days off a week to go stay with my sister and booking visits with the kids at CAS (Children's Aid Society). She was allowed to have supervised visits, so I made sure I was able to go with her each time.

My family meant everything to me, and my niece and nephew were so special and needed us— they needed their Mom and their family. Losing them was not an option!! As the months went on, I helped my sister apply for more permanent housing through the system. We did our best to enjoy the short visits we were granted with the kids, but leaving them was always so difficult. We brought stuffed toys and coloring books from their Mom, so they had good memories to carry them to their next visit. We went shopping and I made sure her cupboards were full, she had food in the refrigerator and stocked her up with toiletries and things for the kids, so they (CAS) could see she could care for her children when they came back home to my sister. As the weeks passed, court dates kept being pushed back, my sister began to lose hope that she would ever get her children back. I did my best to encourage her to stay positive, saying to her, "You just need to show them that you CAN care for them. You can do this!"

Unconditional Love

Apparently, my encouragement wasn't enough. One evening my sister called me and she barely said "Hello", before launching into what would be another life-changing conversation. She said, "Heather, I just don't know if I have it in me. I can't give my kids what they need." Then she asked, "Would you take my kids for me? I know you would be a great Mom to them, you have been such a good Aunt." I was stunned. I froze and for the first time since this ordeal began, I knew she was done fighting for her kids. Not because she wanted to be, but it was clear she wasn't sure how to.

"Oh Dianne, I will... if that's what it comes to, but you can still get them back!!" We can still...

"No, it's over Heather. The courts don't feel I am fit to take care of them..."

I don't even remember how that call ended... but eventually, it did. I sobbed for hours that night. What now? How would I talk to Jamie (who was my boyfriend at the time) about this? In the few days that followed though, I decided that no matter what I had to do, we would not lose the kids– whatever it took, I was ready!!

Jamie and I had been dating now for about a year, but this was no time to have a conversation about kids. How would this work? What would we say to his family?

Well, we did have the conversation in August 2006 (I believe it was). There was no doubt in my mind, what I needed to do. However, it didn't seem fair to drag him into this, so I gave him an out. To be honest, although I loved him at this point, I wanted him to know that I would completely understand if he needed to walk away.

He paused and was quiet for a long time. "No way, no way you are doing this on your own. We have come too far and I love you, no matter what. Let's do this!" Well, isn't that an interesting turn of events!! Yes, within a couple of weeks, we were driving to meet with my sister and her Social Worker, and see what our next steps were.

Within the next month, we had our house rented out. We decided to rent a condo in the city, so we could live closer to work and set sail on the most intense journey of our lives yet!

Interviews, assessments, police checks, more assessments, multiple questionnaires, surprise visits, we had to attend a weekly program over 9 months, learning about becoming parents to children who were in the system. It would be a long road ahead, but we were ready and willing to do this– together! We had amazing support, compassion and love from everyone we knew. Our co-workers, our bosses, friends, family members and our parents too. It was incredible to have such support and God knows, we needed it.

On January 6, 2007, Jamie proposed to me while we walked one night. It was the sweetest proposal... under a street light. At first I responded, "What?" Then quickly followed it with a teary-eyed, "Yes" and a sarcastic, "Really, now?!" We stood there for a while and I hugged Jamie so tight. I was truly in love with this man. We were embarking on an incredible journey that would mean making a GIANT change in our life as we knew it. That's US– adventurers at heart, and we both love, unconditionally!

Do the Right Thing

Now we were planning a wedding, working through the logistics of adopting two children, buying a house (a condition of getting the children), and we were both working full-time jobs. We had started going and picking up the children and caring for them, three days a week in March of 2007.

On the evening of March 8th, 2007, my sister and I spoke and she said, "I am so happy they are going to be loved and cared for."

I pleaded with her to continue with calls and visits (as per the agreement). I was heartbroken that she couldn't have her children with her, but I knew it was the right thing for her and for the children. I didn't know it then, but that would be the last conversation I would have with my sister. Sadly, to this day, we still have had no call or contact of any kind— despite reaching out and trying to find her. I miss her terribly, but there must be a reason why and suppose it's best not to question God's plan.

On July 1, 2007 we went to pick up the children. We were going home with them permanently. It was a tough day, a teary goodbye as they left their wonderful Foster Mom, but that's why they did the transition over a four-month period. After a few extra reassuring hugs and their favorite teddy bears to snuggle with, we were on our way. About an hour into the trip back to our place, the children asked if we had some snacks. We stopped for a picnic lunch and exchanged smiles and hugs – we loved them so much!! I kept my sunglasses on, as I fought back tears of sadness and joy all at the same time. I call it an emotional tug-of-war... wanting things to be different, but knowing that these children deserved so much more. It was such an emotional time for all of us, but it was truly the right thing to do. The kids were with us, their family and by us proceeding with adoption, it also meant the two kids wouldn't be separated, which is always a risk with siblings in foster care. This was not an option— they needed each other and their family.

On January 12th, 2008, Jamie and I were married, and we included our children in the wedding party, of course! We even exchanged rings with the kids, as a symbol of our commitment to them and all of us becoming a family.

The next couple of years proved challenging, in a good way as we all learned to live and grow together. They were doing well in school and it was an adjustment, but they were doing well and the adoption was set to be finalized in April 2010.

We loved it where we were living, but found we were in the car driving back and forth many weekends to visit or attend events with our family and friends. So, while the kids were still young enough, we decided that it was time to move back to be close to our families and our friends. We knew this would be another adjustment, but one that would actually provide more stability and long-term roots for our children— they needed that and we desperately wanted them to have stability, strong family roots and for them to know they are loved.

In February 2010, I landed my dream job— a facilitator in training and development. There would be some travel, but I would work from home and be around more for the children as well. In April 2010, two amazing things happened... the adoption was finalized and Jamie landed a job downtown. Everything was lining up perfectly, we could both take the train to our offices, which meant no commuting on the highway.

Later that year, we had also started trying again for a child. Yes, now that we had moved, we both loved our jobs and we felt the children were settled, the adoption was final, and it was time. It took a while, but in March 2011, I found out I was expecting which was funny timing, as we had booked a trip to Disney in California as our big family trip. What a great trip it was. Although morning sickness had begun which made things interesting, we had the best time. None of us had ever been to Disneyland, so it was truly a magical 3 days for us all. We then drove out to Palm Springs where we shared an amazing week with Jamie's parents, rented a beautiful California home with a pool and had an incredible and memorable holiday.

It was a busy time, preparing for a new baby, going through more changes with our jobs and with the kids. We did our best to spend lots of quality time with them and let them know that the baby would keep us busy, but we would let the kids be involved as much as possible. Good thing too, because things were about to ramp up, sooner than we thought!!

Perseverance

On October 24th, 2011 at 2:50 p.m., my water broke, 40 minutes before our family photo session. I called my midwife and she said that if I felt okay, I could go and do our family pictures. However, we would be having our baby within 24 hours. I immediately called my boss to let him know I was likely going to deliver our baby tonight. As for our family photos, it was a bit late to cancel and I did feel okay... no laboring or pain. So we went and had our family pictures taken. We finished up though, and my husband whispered to me, "How are you feeling? Are you okay? Your belly seems to be quite a bit lower than before." He was right, I had dropped, but probably because I had lost so much of my water. On the way home though, I knew something was up. It had just occurred to me that our baby hadn't moved in the last couple of hours. When we got home, I started calling around to get my class covered for the next day, as I was supposed to teach a workshop. Finally, a colleague answered at just after 5:00 p.m. I was covered.

We called our midwife again to let her know that we hadn't felt our baby move. She reassured us that with so much of my water gone, there probably wasn't a lot of room for him to move like he used to. She suggested that I have some juice, crunch on some ice and go to a quiet room to rest. I wasn't in labor, so it would likely be too early to go to the hospital. "Okay", I said and hung up the phone. I started sobbing and said to my husband, "Something doesn't feel right. He has moved 24/7 and now nothing. My husband was equally concerned, knowing this was unusual and called our midwife back. She agreed to meet us at the hospital within the hour. Jamie and I both kept our cool, packed up the car and the kids and made our way to the hospital. My in-laws picked up our two children at the hospital, and Jamie wheeled me in. Our mid-wife arrived very soon after us. She assured us that he was at 37 weeks and that he was a good size. She encouraged me to stay calm and to breathe. I did and I was.

Around 7:30 p.m., I was ushered into a room and put on a monitor. "Ah yes, there's your baby heartbeat – good." The OB did a few tests and the usual checks. I was laboring, mostly back labor (argh), but she said I wasn't dilating, I was only at 2 cm. Two hours went by, she checked again – nothing had changed. The OB said she didn't feel as though I could deliver naturally and urged me to consider a Caesarian Section. I looked at my midwife and she agreed that given my condition, I should consider this as the best option. I still wasn't dilating. Although I was hoping to deliver naturally, and have that wonderful experience, I wasn't about to put our baby's life in danger. So, I nodded, "Okay, if you think that's best, let's do that." No sooner, had I nodded, suddenly our baby's heart-rate plummeted and in a flash, a team of nurses and the OB came rushing in. They shoved a clipboard into my hand and said, "Sign here please...

we have to go now!!!" The nurses flipped me around, trying to get our baby's heart-rate to come back. Time seemed to stand still. I heard them say, "Sorry, you can't come in here." I saw them hold Jamie back and he calmly, but firmly called out, "it's going to be okay!"

In the operating room, they were about to put me out with a general anesthetic, but our baby's heart-rate had stabilized so they said they could do a spinal. Because I was awake for the procedure, they were able to bring Jamie in. He was suited up in scrubs and immediately came to check on me. I felt super calm. My midwife was there with me through the spinal injection and talked me through the procedure. I was okay.

At 10:38 p.m., on Monday, October 24th, our beautiful baby boy was born, just 6lbs, 1oz, but feisty and cried as if to say, "I am here world– look out!!" It was love at first sight!! He had the most gorgeous black curls and I couldn't wait to hold him. First they had to stitch me up and then... they put him on my chest. Jamie smiled and we both snuggled him. He was perfect!

As it turned out, Ethan was in distress. The OB said it was good we went in when we did. The umbilical cord was wrapped around both his neck and his little belly, which explained his heartrate dropping and him not moving over the last few hours. We were in the hospital for 5 days, as Ethan's weight dropped to 5 lbs 8oz. It was a tough few days, but Ethan starting nursing well, and eventually his weight was back up over 6lbs. Yay, we were going home!

Resilience

On Monday, October 31st, our friends came over. Amanda couldn't wait to snuggle Ethan and it was nice to visit. Our husbands' took our kids out for trick or treating while we sipped tea and chatted. About an hour passed, and I noticed my one eye was watering a lot, almost burning. I also noticed, as did my friend, that I was drooling. She looked at me and said, "What is happening? Are you okay?" My face felt numb, and the more I tried to blink and rub my eye, the more it burned. I went and got a cold cloth and we just sat until our husband's returned. Later that night, I couldn't see well and my eye burned. Jamie got me settled with Ethan and I sat and nursed him while he looked up what could be happening. I slept with a cold cloth over my eye, well what bit of sleep I could get between nursing every two hours!

The next day, my condition worsened and the right side of my face was drooping very noticeably now, and the numbness had spread from my forehead down to my neck. My husband insisted that we go to the doctor. From what he read, I had Bell's Palsy and if caught early enough, within 24-48 hrs, treatment could be administered and serious, more permanent nerve damage reduced.

The doctor confirmed it was in fact Bell's Palsy and said, that we had likely caught it in time. He prescribed medication for the virus that was causing the nerve damage, ointment and instructed me to tape my eye shut every night to sleep. He explained that with Bell's Palsy, the muscles that allow my eye to open and close had been attacked. So, without being able to blink and tear, my eye was drying out which is why my eye felt scratchy and burned. I was also referred to a Massage Therapist, Jane who specialized in and treated me with both myofascial release, cranial sacral therapy and laser treatments twice a week for eight weeks. Jane was a miracle worker! Eventually I regained most of the feeling in my face, and today, even though

I can see it and still feel minimal numbness, most people cannot tell that I had Bell's Palsy.

After the treatments were complete, things returned to normal again. I could close my eye again, so nursing every two hours at night became a bit easier. We started building good routines. I loved being at home with my children and life was good.

Follow your Heart

Things were changing drastically in my department though and there was talk of reorganizing the team, our clientele and the way we would do business. All through my maternity leave, I started thinking of business ideas and how to start my own business. My ideas ranged from Mama`s Spaghetti Sauce, to Sewing with Love, opening a Home Daycare... until I got the call about a promotion. Yes, my director called me that summer before I was to return to work, offering me a promotion and informing me of all the changes that were taking place. Now I had a tough decision to make. Jamie and I talked that night, and the night after that. I was struggling with going back to work in some ways, knowing that I would be traveling more with my new position. We had three children now, a one-year-old, a 7-year-old and a 9-year-old, AND I was going to travel. This was going to be yet another big adjustment.

A big adjustment was an understatement. The travel came fast and furious. I really loved my work, being back in the classroom and getting certified to teach a number of new programs. In January 2013, a couple of colleagues and I began doing our Coach Training. I loved it and quickly realized, I had a passion for Coaching and looked forward to working with clients in the coming months once I had completed my training. I started putting the word out and very quickly, I had people who immediately came forward to be my first clients during my 8-Month Coaching Practicum. Hmm, now I was on to something. I knew in my heart of hearts, that this coaching and training job might not be sustainable, but starting my own practice could be an incredible business. I rolled with the tides over the next few months, but the waters got very rough. At home, my husband was holding the fort more than ever and that was not easy, given his work in the IT (Information Technology) world.

We were busier than ever and it was wearing on us all. I took a week off that summer and realized how much I missed being with my children. I was traveling pretty much every week and growing tired of living out of a suitcase. I was really loving the coaching practicum and I enjoyed working with my "clients", so over the next few months, I worked hard at completing my Coaching Practicum. In December, 2013, it was official, I had my coaching designation! I was thrilled and the wheels also began turning in my mind.

On a personal note, I was not well. During Christmas break I went to see my doctor who said I had walking pneumonia and said I needed to start taking better care of myself. My doctor prescribed me with a Steroid inhaler and suggested I take it for about 8 weeks. In my heart, I knew that my illness was driven by emotion; being away so much and a lack of passion for my job— I loved my work, but no longer loved this job. I was missing my family terribly, all of which was contributing to my declining performance at work. In the classroom, I felt good. I was getting good reviews, but I started talking very openly with my manager and my team about missing my family. I stopped booking myself for extensive travel.

On December 24th, yes, Christmas Eve, I was through living this way, or rather existing this way. My husband and I were talking in the kitchen and suddenly, I found myself sobbing uncontrollably.

"I can't do this job anymore!! I hate the travel, I miss you and the kids. I need to find another job soon or I am going to quit!!"

My husband looked at me, poured me a glass of wine and said, "Really? Well, let's talk about this for a minute." He continued, after a long pause, "To be honest, I would never have said anything because I know you love your work, but it has been pretty tough this past year." The next few words he spoke, struck me like a knife in my heart... "I'm not sure we'll make it, if we don't change something soon."

Oh gosh, not sure we'll make it?!! I didn't have to ask what he meant. He had been under a lot of pressure at work, juggling everything at home— with the kids every night (because I was gone all the time, pretty much weekly), meaning he was doing drop-offs and pick-ups every day!

Splitting up our family— DEFINITELY not an option!! Over the next two weeks, I was off with my kids for the Christmas holidays and it was heaven! Now, I was on a mission to figureout how to make this happen— leave my job, my corporate career of almost 17 years. It was time to lead with my heart and start the next chapter in my life!

Over the next couple of weeks, Jamie and I worked out a solid plan and drafted my resignation letter. I had the conversation with my boss and let her know I was choosing my family. I had to. My heart wasn't in it and I wasn't performing at my best anymore. I would fulfill any commitments I had up to then, but February 28th would be my last day.

Wow, it was over. A lengthy and successful career, lots of amazing opportunities and promotions... then poof!! Just like that, I was on a new path. A new chapter... no wait, a completely new series was beginning. It was time to break the mould and create a new one. Yes, I was leaving my career and I was starting over, but for all the right reasons– my family. True love.

Well, I did move on and quickly! About two months after resigning, I was looking into how to grow my coaching practice, I started networking – I was fully entering the world of entrepreneurship. How was I feeling? Ah, terrified, but mostly super excited!

Oh and I started running again, eating and sleeping better. Within 2 months, I was able to stop taking that steroid inhaler– I felt like a weight had been lifted, I could breathe!

Fast forward to July 2017, almost three years in business and I have never looked back, not even for a moment! I truly believe my faith and a few guiding principles were the key; unconditional love, do the right thing, perseverance, resilience and follow your heart.

Afraid? Absolutely, fear was and continues to be part of my journey. However, the best way I can explain it is that at one point, my desire to step through the fear, despite it, became stronger. I realized I can step through fear because I know what I need to do. There was a point where I came into my own. Knowing my "Why", loving unconditionally and staying true to my values helped me make many tough decisions and kept me focused even through the dark days. It also helped me understand my purpose. Yes, I believe that all of the things I have gone through in my life, were positioning me for both of my roles now.

Finally, I am living my passion and my purpose— I was born to be an entrepreneur, but more importantly, I was born to be a Mom!

Heather Wilson is a Corporate Trainer and Leadership Coach, Founder of Spark Your Vitality. Her passion is promoting healthy communication in the workplace and helping others recognize their potential, plan it out and fulfill their dreams. Heather is married and a mother of three beautiful children.

*Authors from **The Sisterhood folios: Live Out Loud** speak about their experience.*

So glad I was part of that experience. I thank you . Making a whole new group of friends is sweet. Then to reach #1 was way over the top of emotions. Totally surpassed my expectations. I have and would recommend to friends and anybody who is thinking of writing a book or a chapter in a book to call Creative Publishing Group. They treated me with respect and honesty. Very professional. I am no longer afraid and I feel confident for the next book. Warrior onward.
~Teresa Ursini

Thank you both for everything. I had a wonderful experience and when I am ready to publish my own book I will definitely be reaching out to you.
~Jennifer Febel

I loved the overall experience. Writing was incredible therapy for me and helped me overcome my fears of getting some of my story out there. Carol was outstanding. Attention to every single detail nothing was forgotten. To be honest she made this experience for me. Overall the experience has been amazing and I will for sure be doing it again.
~Claudine Pereira

This has been an amazing, wonderful experience! I'm hoping to do a lot more writing! I'm researching magazines, contests, and I have a solo project in mind!
I will always be grateful for your guidance, encouragement and professionalism!
Can't say enough Carol and Amir!
~Lucy Colangelo

WHAT IS YOUR STORY?

Have you ever said, "I should write my story"?
Is writing a book on your Bucket List?
Do you realize, that by sharing your journey,
you are helping yourself and others?
Impart your wisdom and make a difference!
This will give you a taste for writing
without the pressure of an entire book!
Are you ready to write your own book?
We also do SOLO AUTHOR projects.

The next volume in
The Sisterhood *folios:*

**Ingite Your
Inner Warrior**

The first volume in
Women Think Business –

The Balancing Act

Dear Me – **Notes to my Younger Self**
Experiences, thoughts and lessons
I wish I could share with my younger self.

Inquire about contributing a chapter.

info@creativepublishinggroup.com
www.creativepublishinggroup.com

CPSIA information can be obtained
at www.ICGtesting.com
Printed in the USA
LVHW01s0054011017
550603LV00002B/2/P

9 780995 881068